I0819797

Pseudo-Seneca: *Octavia*

COMPANIONS TO GREEK AND ROMAN TRAGEDY

Series Editor: Thomas Harrison

Aeschylus: Agamemnon, Barbara Goward
Aeschylus: Eumenides, Robin Mitchell-Boyask
Aeschylus: Libation Bearers, C. W. Marshall
Aeschylus: Persians, David Rosenbloom
Aeschylus: Prometheus Bound, I. A. Ruffell
Aeschylus: Seven Against Thebes, Isabelle Torrance
Aeschylus: Suppliants, Thalia Papadopoulou
Euripides: Alcestis, Niall W. Slater
Euripides: Andromache, Hanna M. Roisman
Euripides: Bacchae, Sophie Mills
Euripides: Children of Heracles, Florence Yoon
Euripides: Cyclops, Carl A. Shaw
Euripides: Electra, Rush Rehm
Euripides: Hecuba, Helene P. Foley
Euripides: Heracles, Emma Griffiths
Euripides: Hippolytus, Sophie Mills
Euripides: Ion, Lorna Swift
Euripides: Iphigenia at Aulis, Pantelis Michelakis
Euripides: Medea, William Allan
Euripides: Orestes, Matthew Wright
Euripides: Phoenician Women, Thalia Papadopoulou
Euripides: Suppliant Women, Ian Storey
Euripides: Trojan Women, Barbara Goff
Pseudo-Seneca: Hercules on Oeta, George W. M. Harrison
Seneca: Hercules Furens, Neil W. Bernstein
Seneca: Medea, Helen Slaney
Seneca: Oedipus, Susanna Braund
Seneca: Phaedra, Roland Mayer
Seneca: Thyestes, Peter Davis
Sophocles: Antigone, Douglas Cairns
Sophocles: Ajax, Jon Hesk
Sophocles: Electra, Michael Lloyd
Sophocles: Oedipus at Colonus, Adrian Kelly
Sophocles: Philoctetes, Hanna Roisman
Sophocles: Women of Trachis, Brad Levett

Pseudo-Seneca: *Octavia*

Erica M. Bexley

BLOOMSBURY ACADEMIC
LONDON • NEW YORK • OXFORD • NEW DELHI • SYDNEY

BLOOMSBURY ACADEMIC
Bloomsbury Publishing Plc, 50 Bedford Square, London, WC1B 3DP, UK
Bloomsbury Publishing Inc, 1359 Broadway, New York, NY 10018, USA
Bloomsbury Publishing Ireland, 29 Earlsfort Terrace, Dublin 2, D02 AY28, Ireland

First published in Great Britain 2026

Cover image: Giovanni Muzzioli, *Poppea Brings the Head of Octavia to Nero*, 1876. Archivio fotografico del Museo Civico di Modena

A catalogue record for this book is available from the British Library.

Library of Congress Control Number: 2025943274.

ISBN: HB: 978-1-3501-2184-3
ePDF: 978-1-3501-2186-7
eBook: 978-1-3501-2185-0

Series: Companions to Greek and Roman Tragedy

Typeset by RefineCatch Limited, Bungay, Suffolk

For product safety-related questions contact productsafety@bloomsbury.com.

For Omniprop

Contents

Acknowledgements

This little book has incurred debts of gratitude disproportionate to its size. Many thanks are owed to Alice Wright, Zoë Osman and Lily Mac Mahon of Bloomsbury Academic for guiding me throughout the process and remaining patient when I overshot the agreed submission deadline (several times). I am also grateful to Stephanie Fleischmann for sharing with me her then unpublished libretto of *Poppaea*; this was a fascinating opera that I thoroughly enjoyed listening to, reading and writing about. I am likewise indebted to my Higher Latin 3A class of 2023–4, with whom I read *Octavia* in Michaelmas Term: you were a truly superb group of students, from whom I learned much, and whose insight into the text constantly surprised and delighted me. Durham Classics provided – as always – a supportive intellectual environment, and special thanks are due to Giulia Bonasio for correcting my Italian (all remaining errors are obstinately mine). Invitations to present my work at Reading, Durham and HU Berlin were gratefully received and proved immensely enriching experiences. Finally, I want to thank my family: Ioannis, for listening to my ideas, adding his own, being a most attentive reader of my work and never flagging in his support, and Daphne and Marcus, for bringing such joy. The last word here goes to Omniprop Inc, an influence from the distant past, without which I might never have discovered the wonders of theatre: I dedicate this book to you.

1

Octavia and Roman Historical Drama

Octavia is a mystery: its author unknown; its date uncertain; its genre disputed. This compact drama tells the story of Nero's divorce from Octavia, daughter of the emperor Claudius, and his remarriage to the glamorous Poppaea. It is the only surviving Roman play on an historical topic: it features Nero himself, in a tyrannical if remarkably untheatrical role, and Seneca as his beleaguered advisor. It telescopes into three days events that in reality occupied roughly a month: Nero decides on divorce and cannot be dissuaded; he marries Poppaea; the Roman citizenry revolts; Octavia is sent into exile. Looming large in the background is the cyclical, intrafamilial aggression of the Julio-Claudian dynasty, due to which Messalina falls victim to Claudius, Claudius to Agrippina, and Agrippina to Nero. No one, not even the chorus, expects this violence to cease, and the play ends on a pessimistic note as Octavia proceeds into exile, anticipating only death. Onto this historical frame the playwright has woven material from Greek and Roman tragedy: Octavia resembles Sophocles' Electra and Antigone, while Seneca, ominously, plays the role of his own Thyestes. History becomes tragedy and tragedy history, dissolving distinctions between fiction and non-fiction. *Octavia* is an enjoyable pastiche, loosely if reverently modelled on Senecan drama and revelling in the lurid lives of Rome's imperial family. But who wrote this play? When? And to what purpose? There are no easy answers.

1.1 Authorship and date

Octavia's origins are obscure. The play survived antiquity by being attached to a manuscript of eight Senecan tragedies. This incorporation most likely occurred in the fourth/fifth century CE when codices replaced scrolls, and many new editions of classical works were consequently issued in codex form.[1] This was an era characterized by eager, anxious efforts to recover and preserve literature from the preceding centuries, and it is not hard to see how, in such a context, *Octavia* came to be grouped with a collection of Seneca's genuine plays and another spurious work in Senecan style, the tragedy *Hercules Oetaeus*. This group of texts, *Octavia* included, was subsequently copied and transmitted in what is now referred to as the 'A' branch of Senecan manuscripts. Seneca was tacitly accepted as the author of the entire collection until at least the fourteenth century, when early Italian humanists began to query *Octavia*'s attribution.

The case against Senecan authorship is now well established, chiefly because *Octavia* alludes to events that happened after Seneca's death,[2] and because the playwright's writing style is generally agreed to differ from Seneca's, lacking the punch and visual intensity of his language while displaying a non-Senecan regard for form and scenic arrangement.[3] Owing to the accident of its transmission, however, it is still published alongside Seneca's genuine tragedies and classified among his pseudonymously attributed works. In other words, *Octavia* cannot really be separated from Seneca even if he was not its playwright.

A few alternative authors have been proposed, all of them roughly contemporary with Seneca. Annaeus Cornutus, Stoic philosopher and teacher of Lucan and Persius, is one candidate. His authorship has been suggested[4] because of a dubious line in the *Life of Persius* that describes Cornutus as 'at that time a tragedian of the Stoic school' (*illo tempore tragicus sectae Stoicae*). But the line is omitted from modern editions for being either corrupt or a gloss on the text, making Cornutus an unlikely option. Another candidate is Curiatus Maternus, a playwright and ex-orator of the Vespasianic period portrayed in Tacitus' *Dialogue on Orators*.[5] Tacitus' work opens with Maternus recently having composed an historical drama about Cato (2.1–3.4) and mentions his prior composition of a *Domitius* (3.4). The idea of his also being *Octavia*'s author is nice but fanciful, because Curiatus Maternus cannot be firmly identified in the extant historical record; he may well be Tacitus' invention. A third possibility is Pomponius Secundus, a noted playwright under Claudius who is known to have engaged in debate with Seneca about the finer points of tragic diction. But Secundus' latest attestation is 51 CE, meaning he is unlikely to have written *Octavia*. Further conjecture is impossible; in Anthony Boyle's pithy phrase, *Octavia*'s author 'is neither Seneca nor known'.[6]

As for dating, the play is generally agreed to be post-Neronian, though scholars continue to debate the precise era of its composition. There are three main options: the short reign of Galba that followed immediately upon Nero's suicide (June 68 CE–January 69 CE);[7] the early 70s CE, when Vespasian was in power;[8] or the early 90s CE, under Domitian.[9]

Arguments in favour of the first option, Galba's reign, focus on *Octavia*'s hostile portrayal of Nero and the playwright's accurate knowledge of Nero's court, including the correct use of imperial titles. Familiar, even offhand references to less famous aristocrats from the Claudian and Neronian eras – such as Crispinus, Poppaea's first husband (*Oct.* 713), or Julia Livia, the mother of Rubellius Plautus (*Oct.* 944) – are thought to indicate an author writing in the period just after Nero's death, when the events of his calamitous reign were fresh in people's memories. Further, the play's characterization of Nero as a tyrannous oppressor and enemy of the Roman people complements the historical narrative promulgated by Galba, who sought to portray himself as a liberator, and his reign as a rebirth of quasi-republican liberty. Other links to Galban ideology are the play's potential evocation of slogans also found on Galba's coinage (e.g. *renascens* at *Oct.* 395) and its disapproving hints about Nero's opulence (*Oct.* 427; 433); for Galba, like Vespasian after him, was an advocate of old-fashioned austerity.[10]

The key to this hypothesis is *Octavia*'s anti-Neronian sentiment, which should not be taken for granted, no matter how conventional it may seem to a twenty-first-century audience. For, notwithstanding the rebellion against him, Nero was a popular figure throughout the Roman empire and remained so after his death. His 'legendary' status is confirmed by the strange phenomenon of three impostor 'Neros' who emerged from the eastern provinces and acquired followers in the two decades from 69 to 89 CE.[11] Galba's successor, Otho, recognized this popularity and capitalized on it. He styled himself 'Nero Otho' to establish legitimacy by linking his reign to the last of the Julio-Claudians. His own successor, Vitellius, continued this pro-Neronian trend by performing funeral sacrifices to Nero and ordering the public performance of one of the actor-emperor's songs, which he greeted with rapturous approval. Against this backdrop, Galba's attitude, and that of *Octavia*, stands out. Nero's posthumous reputation was still being contested in 69 CE, and his later demonization was far from guaranteed. Nero had been especially popular with the Roman plebeians: might Galba have commissioned *Octavia* to persuade them of the dead emperor's cruelty? It is not an implausible hypothesis, but there is no evidence to confirm it either. And the brief, chaotic span of Galba's reign (just six months!) makes it unlikely that much imperial attention was devoted to literature.

In fact, the shortness of Galba's time in power is a major reason to doubt *Octavia*'s Galban dating. Galba did not have enough time to establish a firm ideology or promote it via the relevant cultural channels before he, too, met rebellion and a bloody end. *Octavia*'s anti-Neronian sentiment could just as easily belong to the reign of

Vespasian (69–79 CE), who likewise cast himself as a liberator and restorer of the Roman people following Nero's tyranny, and likewise cultivated an ethos of austerity. As for the play's references to specific individuals and use of imperial titles, it is unlikely that these would have been forgotten or muddled only a few years after Nero's death. Some of the individuals in question, like Rubellius Plautus' mother, Julia Livia, actually met their end under Claudius, which meant that they were not such 'recent' history by the time of *Octavia*'s composition in any case. If Julia Livia was significant enough to have been remembered from the time of her suicide in 43 CE to the first possible date of the *Octavia* in 69 CE, surely her presence would not preclude a slightly later dating for the play, in the early 70s?

These factors point favourably towards the second option for dating *Octavia*: the early Flavian period, under Vespasian. This was a time when Nero's posthumous denigration really took hold, as Vespasian's programmes of civic and financial recovery promulgated ideas of Nero's ruinous self-interest and excess. Vespasian advertized himself as returning Rome to the Romans, the most obvious example being his foundation of the Colosseum on land previously occupied by the pleasure gardens of Nero's Golden House. The idea was that private luxury had been reclaimed as a space for mass public entertainment.[12] *Octavia*'s largely sympathetic portrayal of the Roman citizenry and concomitant condemnation of Nero fit well within this context. Further, Vespasian's overt sponsorship of Roman writers, whose works were employed to strengthen his position as *princeps*,[13] increases the likelihood of *Octavia*'s being composed in this period. Evidence from Tacitus' *Dialogue on Orators* (2.1–3.4) certainly suggests that other plays on historical topics were being written and recited in Vespasianic Rome, though these claims are impossible to verify.

Alongside Nero's posthumous reputation, Seneca's is also relevant to *Octavia*'s date of composition because the work is, inter alia, a homage to Seneca's tragic style. Vengeful ghosts, determined tyrants, ineffectual advisors, passion-restraint scenes and the protagonist's troubled opening monologue: all of these classically Senecan elements feature, remixed and reimagined, in *Octavia*. Quintilian in *The Orator's Education* (10.1.125) recalls that when he was active as a teacher of rhetoric under the Flavians, Seneca 'was virtually the only author in young men's hands'. Though Quintilian doubtless has Seneca's prose style uppermost in his mind – why else would he have tried to moderate its influence? – it is still reasonable to assume that this aesthetic preferment extended to all of Seneca's works, including those written for the stage. But Seneca's popularity appears to have waned by the time of Trajan and the Antonines, displaced first by the neo-Ciceronian ethos of Quintilian and the Younger Pliny, and later by the antiquarianism of Gellius and Fronto. Hence, Quintilian's *The Orator's Education*, published *c.* 95 CE, represents a strong *terminus ante quem* for dating *Octavia*, as an era in which Seneca's work was valued and imitated.

The case for an early Flavian dating looks good – or rather, it looks as good as it can given the limited, often sketchy nature of the evidence and the perils involved in dating any work by internal clues alone. But we need also to consider the third proposition, that *Octavia* was written in the late 80s/early 90s, under Domitian.

The mainstay of this hypothesis is a few similarities between *Octavia* and Statius' *Silvae*, a collection of occasional poetry of which the first three books appear to have been published in 93 CE. Noted first by Rudolf Helm[14] and explored further by Rolando Ferri in his 2003 commentary on the play,[15] these parallels are slight and remain contested.[16] The first is the nurse comparing Octavia's sufferings to Juno's endurance of Jupiter's affairs (*Oct.* 201–18), which bears mild resemblance to *Silvae* 1.2.130–6, a catalogue of affairs and betrayals the ends with Juno ensuring Jupiter's fidelity. The second is a favourable comparison between Poppaea's beauty and Helen's (*Oct.* 773–5), the phrasing of which may find a parallel in *Silvae* 1.2.262–5. More broadly, *Silvae* 1.2 and *Octavia* 690–711 resemble each other in their retrospective descriptions of marriage celebrations. Recalling the event in a series of flashbacks is an original technique, featuring chiefly in Statius and *Octavia* and suggesting an intertextual relationship between them.[17]

However, these parallels are not strong enough to carry the full weight of the play's dating. They are weak echoes at best, appearing in the generic context of catalogues where many commonplace ideas and phrases are bound to occur. And even if we do grant their significance, we face the further hurdle of ascertaining whether *Octavia* imitated Statius or vice versa. Add to these concerns Domitian's supposed hostility towards criticism of Nero (Pliny *Panegyric* 53.4), and his general paranoia about potential literary denigration of his reign (e.g. Suetonius *Domitian* 10.1), and the likelihood of *Octavia*'s being written during his principate seems slim. It cannot, of course, be discounted, just as a Galban date cannot be, but in the absence of further evidence, Vespasian's reign is the most probable, by reason of the emperor's patronage, his championing of anti-Neronian attitudes, the fact of Nero's reign being recent history and of Seneca's popularity being at its peak. Though a lot of supposition remains, this seems the most defensible option.

There is one final issue involved in *Octavia*'s dating that I have left until last because it deserves separate consideration: the play's potential use of historical sources. There is nothing in the play text that confirms outright the author's memory or personal experience of the events depicted; the accuracy of his/her portrayal may derive from book learning instead. It has been proposed that *Octavia* draws material from the now lost histories of Cluvius Rufus, Fabius Rusticus and the Elder Pliny.[18] Since – the argument goes – the outlines of these histories can be detected in the surviving accounts of Tacitus and Suetonius, and since *Octavia* often follows the sequence of events reported in these later works, the play can plausibly be said to have relied on historical accounts published around the early Flavian period, in some instances as part of Vespasian's programmatic denigration of Nero. This would be further evidence in support of a post-Galban dating. But the hypothesis involves a lot of speculation, first because these Flavian histories no longer exist, and second because the direction of influence is unclear even for the histories that do survive: did *Octavia* borrow (at one remove) from Tacitus, or Tacitus from *Octavia*? A strong case can and has been made for the latter scenario, of Tacitus being acquainted with *Octavia* and incorporating elements of its final lyric scene into his sad summary of Octavia's fate at *Annals* 14.63–4.[19] The implications of this exchange between historical fiction and historiography will be explored fully in the next chapter ('Historical Background'). For now, it suffices to note the radical instability of the historical source material traditionally employed to contextualize *Octavia*. We tend to regard history as something stable and clear, as the more factual, objective yardstick against which fictions like *Octavia* can be measured. Historical narrative is assumed to have a close, almost permeable relationship with reality that fiction supposedly spurns. But this is misleading because historical narrative is comparable to fiction in its delineating of events and consequences, and, more broadly, in being a textual representation and interpretation of the world around it. Though it aims at greater factual content, historiography nonetheless constructs reality, with ancient historians particularly inclined to regard their works as literary enterprises. To the extent, too, that ancient historians cannot be held to modern principles of scholarly detachment, we should be wary of positing too strict a division between *Octavia*'s and, say, Tacitus' account of Nero's divorce. The boundary is pervious, more so given *Octavia*'s status as historical drama: the work already stands at the intersection of factual and fictional material, inviting further interplay between the two.

Octavia, then, is a text unmoored from the standard anchorage of authorship and date. Granted it is not the only work to have been transmitted from antiquity without this information, but its historical content throws the issue into sharper than usual relief. This situation presents the historicizing literary critic – a category to which most Classicists belong – with certain challenges and restrictions: how exactly can we assess the drama's purpose? How might it relate to other works from the same or similar eras? Can any secure pronouncements be made about its political or social significance?[20] The play has often been a magnet for the sort of traditional philological criticism that seeks to solve contextual problems via internal clues and stylistic analysis. But the absence of such details as date and author can also be viewed positively, as an invitation to focus more interpretive energy on the text itself and even, as Tom Geue recently demonstrates, to assess the ways in which pseudonymity augments rather than handicaps *Octavia*'s production of meaning.[21] Viewed from this angle, the play is a post-structuralist's dream:[22] a piece that defies assignation to a single creative authority and that appears to produce rather than merely reflect the historical conditions of its genesis. Whether by design or by the happenstance of transmission, *Octavia* is a prime example of the 'readerly' text that Roland Barthes once hoped would supplant 'writerly' ones.[23] There couldn't be a clearer example of a text's reception and meaning exceeding authorial control.

1.2 The *fabula praetexta*

Octavia's genre is only marginally more secure than its authorship and date. The play's content pulls it into the orbit of the *fabula praetexta*, a Roman genre of historical drama named after the purple-bordered toga worn by magistrates. Existing from the time of Naevius (*c.*

280/260–200 BCE), *praetextae* dealt with subject matter of national significance from Roman legend, like Romulus' achievements, to military heroism and defence of the state, like Brutus' expulsion of Tarquin. *Octavia* shares some characteristics with these earlier plays, but its relationship to them is complicated by its relatively late position in the genre's development and the sheer chance of its being the only Roman historical drama to survive antiquity intact, which raises questions about how representative it is. Further complicating the matter is *Octavia*'s obvious debt to tragedy, from its use of stock tragic characters and scenes – nurse and heroine; tyrant and advisor – to its adaptation of material from Sophocles and Seneca. While not precluding its categorization as a *praetexta*, these tragic features distance *Octavia* from the seemingly celebratory atmosphere of Roman historical drama. Whereas most *praetexta* plays are assumed to have memorialized the Roman past in positive terms, *Octavia* portrays a grim historical episode and ends on a doleful note – perhaps it is really a tragedy in historical guise? The most likely answer is that *Octavia* blends both tragic and historical material, with *fabula praetexta* representing the primary or 'host' genre and tragedy the subordinate or 'guest' genre. But the evidence and arguments deserve careful review before any such hypothesis can be accepted.

Let us begin with the background. Plays on historical topics were not unknown in the Graeco-Roman world. Phrynichus' *Capture of Miletus* (late 490s BCE), which depicted the Persians' sack of the town in 494, is reported to have distressed its audience so much that the poet was fined for reminding Athenians of 'their own evils' (οἰκήια κακά) and the play was banned from performance (Herodotus 6.21.2). It did not survive antiquity. The next major work, which did survive, is Aeschylus' *Persians* (472 BCE), an oblique celebration of Athens' triumph over Xerxes at Salamis, told from the perspective of the defeated. Like *Octavia*, Aeschylus' *Persians* combines tragedy with history. Its influence can also be felt in the Roman tradition of the *fabula praetexta*.[24] A brief summary of its contents will therefore be useful for understanding *Octavia*'s genre and purpose.

Persians opens with a chorus of Persian elders worrying about the war's progress and Xerxes' fate. Xerxes' mother, Atossa, queen and wife of the recently deceased Darius, enters to report a dream vision portending her son's defeat; her exchange with the chorus is interrupted by a messenger bringing news of the Persian disaster; after lengthy questioning, the queen departs to prepare a sacrifice and the chorus, alone on stage, laments and imagines the Persians' naval rout; Atossa returns with ritual offerings and the chorus pronounces a hymn to summon Darius' ghost, who duly appears. Having received the news of his son's downfall, Darius warns against future Greek campaigns and instructs the queen to prepare new robes for Xerxes, who will return in rags; the queen departs again, and the intervening chorus praises Darius before Xerxes enters, alone, in rags, and joins the chorus in a ritual lament that closes the play.

Persians furnishes some instructive parallels with *Octavia*. Both plays adopt a tragic view of history in which anxiety, sadness and hubris predominate. Both also dramatize events that seem grim from the central characters' perspective (Xerxes' defeat; Octavia's divorce and exile), but most likely instilled in the audience a sense of pride and security (because Athens won, because Rome drove out Nero). Like *Persians*, *Octavia* may have served as a cautionary tale, in this case about the evils of unfettered autocracy.[25] Both dramatists use a tragic framework to encapsulate historical teleology, and both contrast the characters' limited knowledge of history with the audience's fully informed hindsight – a gulf in understanding that lasts for the entire play and resembles an extended version of dramatic irony. Of course, *Octavia* differs substantially in its details, but a summary of its plot will in turn be useful for illuminating these parallels.

Octavia begins at dawn, with the eponymous heroine lamenting her family's intergenerational hostilities; her nurse enters the chamber to calm Octavia's fears and advise wifely submission to Nero; Octavia refuses and the scene ends in stalemate. Enter a chorus of Roman citizens: it hopes that the rumour of Nero's impending divorce is baseless, makes clear its support for Octavia and proceeds to deliver a protracted account of Agrippina's murder. The following scene opens with a monologue from Seneca, who regrets his return from exile to serve Nero's tyranny; Nero enters and the two debate the merits of merciful versus aggressive rulership, with Nero outfencing his erstwhile tutor and confirming his plan to marry Poppaea the following day. The scene shifts: it is nearly dawn on the following day and Agrippina's ghost appears, raging against her son and predicting his downfall; the ghost returns to the underworld and Octavia enters, briefly, warning the citizen chorus not to be angry at her fate and hoping, against her better judgement, that divorce will not lead to her death. The angry chorus enters and incites rebellion over Nero's new marriage. The scene shifts again, to the third day in the sequence: an agitated Poppaea tells her nurse about the nightmare that disturbed her sleep the night before and the nurse counters her fears with a positive interpretation of its symbolism; the episode ends with a new chorus, loyal to the regime, singing in praise of Poppaea's beauty. Enter a messenger, with a report of civic unrest, after which the loyalist chorus delivers an ode in praise of Cupid's superior might. Nero returns, with the praetorian prefect in tow: he orders the rebellion to be crushed and Octavia deported and executed; the prefect departs to carry out his mandates. Re-enter the chorus sympathetic to Octavia, which joins the condemned heroine in lamenting her fate and the grim history of her imperial forebears as she departs to certain death on Pandateria. The final lines belong to the chorus: it declares Octavia's fate worse than Iphigenia's and Rome more barbaric than Tauris: there, strangers are slaughtered; in Rome, citizens.

As must be clear from this summary, *Octavia*, like Aeschylus' *Persians*, presents its historical material from the perspective of the defeated. It invites audiences to experience, from a position of safety and victory, the personal toll this event visited upon its victims. The play's tragic vision is situated, paradoxically, in a celebratory framework, its bleak content compensated by a surrounding context of historical optimism, or at the very least, a hope for future stability, whether under Galba or Vespasian. Comparison of *Octavia* and *Persians* also highlights just how proximate a history play is to a tragedy: both genres deal with prominent, powerful individuals; both tend to centre upon disaster; and both situate narratives of personal psychological turmoil against backdrops of socio-political upheaval. Some degree of cross-fertilization is understandable, even expected.[26]

But what about *Octavia*'s relationship to Roman historical drama and what, if any, standard traits can be ascribed to this fragmentary genre? Unlike the Greeks, the Romans recognized history plays as a separate category: Horace praises Roman poets for 'having dared deviate from the footsteps of the Greeks and celebrate domestic deeds in *praetextae* and *togatae*' (*Art of Poetry* 286–8). The latter was a species of light drama, popular in mid-Republican Rome and centred upon the domestic affairs of the extended Roman family, its performance likely distinguished by actors wearing the toga as opposed to the Greek *pallium* seen on the Plautine and Terentian stage.[27] The former of the two genres mentioned by Horace, the *praetexta*, was the *togata*'s serious counterpart: an elevated dramatic form portraying affairs of state, chiefly military successes and Roman foundation stories. Though encompassing these two subcategories of Roman legend and recent history, the *praetexta* was nonetheless a coherent genre, united by an interest in Roman national identity and support of the *res publica* during a time of radical imperial expansion.[28] Composition of *praetextae* spanned at least 250 years, from Naevius (*c.* 280/260–200 BCE) to the end of the republic, and appears to have persisted, sporadically, under the empire, albeit in an altered format that could accommodate the new autocratic system. Pro-republican sentiments, considered one of the genre's hallmarks,[29] had to be adjusted when Rome became a principate, for fear of the plays' appearing subversive or inviting the ruler's unwelcome scrutiny. This necessary shift in tone, combined with major changes to Roman performance culture in the early principate,[30] may be responsible for the genre's extinction sometime in the first century CE.

Despite occupying a discrete dramatic category, *fabulae praetextae* appear to have claimed a marginal place in the canon of Roman theatre. Only ten titles are known from the republican period and three or four from the principate; the addition of a few disputed works rounds out the list to eighteen at most.[31] Although arguments have been made for a flourishing *unscripted* tradition of Roman historical drama, of which *praetexta* plays are merely an ossified outgrowth, the theory founders on a lack of evidence and has not gained wide acceptance.[32] More likely, the *praetexta* is an occasional genre, associated with marking and commemorating major events on the Roman religious calendar: foundation dates; the expulsion of kings; and significant battles and victories. Historical specificity and the genre's support for prominent contemporaries may have combined to delimit its growth.

The earliest recorded author of a *praetexta* is Gnaeus Naevius (*c.* 280/260–200 BCE), who may have been the genre's originator, innovating in this respect as he did in so many other aspects of drama.[33] He is reported to have written two historical plays: *Clastidium*, about Marcus Claudius Marcellus' victory near the town of Clastidium in 222 BCE, and *Romulus*, which may also have been known by the alternative title *Lupus* ('The Wolf').[34] Two plays are likewise attributed to Ennius (239–169 BCE), with the same balance of military content and Roman legend: *Ambracia*, composed in celebration of Marcus Fulvius Nobilior's successful siege of the city in 189 BCE, and *Sabinae*, which presumably dealt with the rape of the Sabine women. Pacuvius (*c.* 220–130 BCE) wrote one *praetexta*, titled

Paullus, which seems to have celebrated Aemilius Paullus' victory at Pydna in 168 BCE and may have been performed at votive games given in honour of the event. The prolific late-republican dramatist Lucius Accius (170–*c.* 80 BCE) wrote a *Brutus*, about Lucius Junius Brutus liberating Rome from King Tarquin, and a *Decius*, about Publius Decius Mus' *devotio* (a Roman practice of sacrificial suicide to secure military victory) at the battle of Sentinum in 295 BCE.

Accius' *Decius* is sometimes referred to by the alternative title of *Aeneadae* ('The Descendants of Aeneas'), which prompts substantial questions about its content and purpose: was there a genealogical connection between Aeneas and the intended aristocratic recipient of this *praetexta*? Who *was* the intended recipient? And why write about Decius Mus in an era that lacked any notable descendants of this family? Only speculative answers can be given,[35] but the questions themselves are useful for elucidating broader issues about the composition of *fabulae praetextae*, namely the plays' dependence upon aristocratic patrons (were they *always* commissioned?) and whether *praetextae* set in the distant past were intended as oblique praise of notable contemporaries. Using history to reflect on the present was a well-established practice in Roman epic that reached its zenith with Vergil's *Aeneid*; it seems likely that *praetextae*, with their mix of historical and legendary subject matter, employed a similar convention. Accius' *Brutus*, for example, may have been associated with the playwright's patron, D. Junius Brutus Callaecus, consul in 138 BCE, whom it would have eulogized indirectly as a descendant of Brutus the liberator. The play's contemporary relevance extended past Accius' lifetime, too, into Rome's late-republican crisis, where Marcus Junius Brutus, Caesar's assassin, attempted to have it restaged at the Apollonian Games in 44 BCE, presumably as a positive comment on his own recent pro-republican activity. We have here a clear instance of Roman historical drama's entanglement with politics and its link to concurrent events, a link that grew even tighter during Rome's civil war periods, when Gaius Cassius Longinus, Marcus Brutus' co-conspirator, reportedly composed another *Brutus*,[36] and Cornelius Balbus wrote, staged and witnessed his own *Iter* ('Journey') in 43 BCE, a drama depicting his travels in 49 BCE to win over Lucius Lentulus to Caesar's side. Both examples point to the *praetexta*'s role as occasional theatre with strong political connotations.

Fewer *praetextae* are attested during the principate. The playwright Pomponius Secundus, a contemporary of the younger Seneca's, is said to have written an *Aeneas*, and the satirist Persius supposedly attempted a *praetexta* as part of his juvenilia. The leading character of Tacitus' *Dialogue*, Curiatus Maternus, is the author of a *Cato* (*Dial.* 2.1–3.4) and a *Domitius* (*Dial.* 3.4), and while these may be imaginary works – given the character's likely fictionality – nonetheless they suggest the genre's continued popularity and political relevance under the Flavians. *Octavia*'s survival notwithstanding, less is known about imperial *praetextae* than republican ones: their attestations are fewer and less certain. Consequently, it is difficult to evaluate how the genre's earlier characteristics adjusted to Rome's shift in government. Celebration of aristocratic patrons was curtailed under the principate, where Augustus exercised a monopoly over cultural production. Praise for the Roman people and for the *res publica* (in its dual connotations of 'state/body politic' and 'the period of oligarchy preceding the principate') also had to be tempered. It seems, from the scant surviving attestations, that imperial *praetextae* acquired an oppositional character: Maternus' *Cato* and *Domitius* are clearly meant as critiques of those in power; Persius qua satirist is hostile to Rome's status quo; and *Octavia* condemns Nero outright.

Yet *Octavia* also shares characteristics with the earlier, republican tradition of historical drama. The play's innovative treatment of dramatic time and space, for example, has been hypothesized as a standard feature of the *praetexta* genre, where the span of events required dramatic action to occupy multiple days and locales.[37] Unlike tragedy, which typically occupies a single day and place,[38] *Octavia*'s plot covers three days – the day before, the day of and the day after Nero and Poppaea's wedding – and moves location through different chambers of the imperial palace to the final scene near the harbour, where Octavia is dragged into exile. Similar fluidity of dramatic time and place occurs in Accius' *Brutus*, which features a speech by Lucretia, presumably at Collatia (*Brut.* 39W), by Tarquin, presumably at Ardea (*Brut.* 17–28 *TRF*[2]), and by an unknown speaker following Tarquin's expulsion, presumably in Rome (*Brut.* 39 *TRF*[2]).[39] Balbus' *Iter* is another likely example, because a play about a *journey* must, by its very nature, have encompassed more than a single day and location.

Another feature *Octavia* seems to share with earlier *praetexta* traditions is its sympathetic portrayal of the Roman citizenry as a prominent force in politics. The first of the play's two choruses, representing the *populus Romanus*, is outspoken in its hatred of Nero, its dismay over Rome's present government and its desire to effect change; it cites republican models of civic duty, especially the expulsion of kings (*Oct.* 291–4), as motivation for combatting Nero's tyranny. Its subsequent rebellion, avowed at 685–89 and reported by the messenger at 780–805, is treated as a laudable enterprise despite its failed outcomes. The play also condemns Nero's disregard for popular sentiment, not only through the character of Seneca, who cautions the emperor against authoritarianism, but also through the audience's implicit knowledge of Nero's eventual overthrow. Hindsight reveals the failure of Nero's autocratic solipsism even though the play's immediate events imply its triumph. In this regard, *Octavia* represents a clever innovation on the pro-republican themes of earlier *praetextae*, expressing its support for the *populus Romanus* in retrospect, and framing its oppositional content not as anti-principate but, more specifically, as anti-Nero.

One final aspect that may evoke the *praetexta* tradition is *Octavia*'s long view of history, which expands beyond Nero's reign to encompass multiple episodes from the republican and monarchical past: Verginia (295–9); Lucretia (300–3); Tullia (305–8); Brutus and Caesar (498–502); Octavian and Antony's proscriptions (503–13); Philippi and Actium (514–22); the Gracchi (882–6); and Livius Drusus (887–90). All these events are treated as paradigmatic, used to reflect on or justify the present in a manner more reminiscent of historiography than of theatre. The same holds true for *Octavia*'s vision of Julio-Claudian genealogy as a recurrent sequence of intrigue, retributive murder and female suffering, with Octavia standing at its miserable conclusion. While such family paradigms also play a prominent role in Senecan tragedy, where they are likewise framed as sources of motivation/justification for the crimes of the present,[40] *Octavia*'s references are more multi-layered and denser; they indicate a deep, sustained engagement with the historical record, a likely trait of the *fabula praetexta* that celebrated singular historical episodes as both paradigmatic and indicative of Rome's socio-cultural continuity.

If these factors suggest *Octavia*'s viable – though far from decisive – association with traditions of Roman historical drama, the play's use of tragedy complicates matters. Its author was clearly well versed in Greek drama, especially Sophocles, whose *Electra* provides a model for *Octavia*'s opening scene. Like the sorrowing Sophoclean heroine, Octavia commences her lament at the approach of dawn (*Oct.* 1–6; *El.* 86–91); grieves for her murdered father (*Oct.* 25–33; *El.* 94–102 and 132–3); compares herself to Procne (*Oct.* 8–9; *El.* 107–9 and 147–9); and longs for an absent brother (*Oct.* 67–9 and 115–24; *El.* 164–72). Her exchange with the nurse, with its mix of iambic and anapestic meters, recalls Electra's with the chorus (*El.*121–327). Both heroines mention having to hide their grief for fear of reprisals (*Oct.* 65–7; *El.* 285–6) and both intend to mourn indefinitely (*semper* at *Oct.* 10 and 167; *El.* 103–6) – a stance that proves truer for Octavia than for Electra. Similarity between the two women's stories is also acknowledged outright at *Octavia* 59–64, where the play's protagonist claims to have surpassed Electra's misfortune, because Electra could hope for her brother Orestes' return, but Octavia's brother, Britannicus, is dead (*Oct.* 67–9). Octavia's claim to 'repeat/recall [Electra's] griefs' (*repetam luctos, Electra, tuos, Oct.* 59) can even be read metapoetically, as the playwright's claim to revisit and outdo his Sophoclean model.[41]

Other evocations of Attic tragedy include Sophocles' *Antigone* in the play's final scene (again, an instance of female lament), and comparison with Iphigenia in Aulis and Tauris (*Oct.* 971–82) as possible references to Euripides. Senecan tragedy claims a strong presence, as well, with the confrontation between Seneca and Nero (*Oct.* 377–592) obviously modelled on Atreus' exchange with his minister in *Thyestes* 176–335. Of course, these intertexts need not dictate the play's genre, but they do make the issue murkier. Muddying the waters still further are the prominent roles *Octavia* assigns to women and the play's emphasis on ritualized sorrow, both characteristic of tragedy. Terminology also gives us pause: Maternus in Tacitus' *Dialogue* calls his historical dramas *tragoediae* ('tragedies') not *praetextae* (*Dial.* 2.1; 3.4).

However, such evidence is not enough to support *Octavia*'s absolute categorization as a tragedy, and scholarly attempts to call it such are largely outdated.[42] The very fact of the play's dealing with historical material, in a culture that granted historical drama its own genre, implies *Octavia*'s close relationship to the *fabula praetexta*. It may not be the most representative instance, but, in Toph Marshall's words, 'to divorce the single example from the sample because of presumed aberrations or deviation from a preconceived genre definition seems self-defeating.'[43] While earlier *praetextae* seem chiefly to have celebrated male achievement in military and political spheres, nothing precluded women's prominence in these earlier plays (what about Ennius' *Sabine Women*?), nor the depiction of sorrowful events. Additionally, interaction with tragedy may be taken as confirmation rather than refutation of the play's status as a *praetexta*, since the two genres were always closely associated in ancient Rome: from Ennius onwards, it was tragedians who composed *praetextae*, while similarities in the two genres' content afforded obvious opportunities for overlap and exchange.[44] Tacitus' Maternus treats his *Cato* and *Thyestes* as contiguous works, the former an historical piece and the latter mythological, but this fluidity need not indicate the *praetexta*'s dissipation under the principate; it may instead signal the genres' ongoing, vital interaction. As demonstrated above, comparison with Aeschylus' *Persians* shows that *Octavia* can be read as an indirect eulogy of Roman achievement. Its ending is not wholly tragic, because the play overall anticipates Nero's defeat and activates audiences' hindsight, inviting them to supplement its content with knowledge of a brighter future. Such interplay between internal and external historical perspectives is intrinsic to all historical fiction; it is something tragedy doesn't do, but *Octavia* does. The play's creative use of historical context, alongside the specific features it shares with earlier *praetextae*, indicate its primary association with the genre: *Octavia* is a *praetexta* first, tragedy second.

1.3 History on stage

Plays demand performance; most are written in expectation of it. Unfortunately for *Octavia*, there is no evidence of its being staged in ancient Rome (if there were, we could date the work!), but there is also little reason to think that it was not or could not be performed in the theatre. Debates about staging versus recitation, which have long plagued Senecan studies,[45] are less applicable to *Octavia*, which exhibits none of Seneca's supposed dramaturgical difficulties: no onstage killing (of humans or animals); no 'running commentaries'; no unannounced entrances and exits. While use of dramatic space is occasionally unclear, and narrative speeches sometimes obstruct the action, *Octavia*'s stage business is not problematic enough to presuppose its being written solely for recital.[46] Granted Tacitus' *Dialogue on Orators* refers to Maternus reciting his *Cato* (*Catonem recitaverat*, *Dial.* 2.1) rather than presenting it in the theatre, but recitation for the purposes of advertisement and peer review prior to publication was common practice in imperial Rome and need not preclude the drama's having been staged later.[47] Another *praetexta* author, Pomponius Secundus, certainly appears to have had his plays performed: Tacitus refers to him as 'putting plays on stage' (*Annals* 11.13, where *carmina* most likely indicates dramatic works) and Pliny tells us that Pomponius, when criticized by friends, replied that he would appeal to the people and make a final decision according to the crowd's applause or silence (*Letters* 7.17.11), which implies a theatrical performance following upon the initial 'trial run' of recitation. *Octavia* belongs in this company and may well have followed the same pattern of development.

Questions of performance context can be answered only speculatively, with inferences made from the earlier *praetexta* tradition. Historical drama in the Roman republic appears to have been staged at *ludi*, festival games that either formed part of the Roman religious calendar or were held, exceptionally, to celebrate a military victory and/or the dedication of a temple.[48] It was common practice for generals to vow *ludi* and temple foundations contingent upon successful campaigns; fulfilment of these vows presented an ideal opportunity for *praetexta* performances. Naevius' *Clastidium* may have been presented at special *ludi* in 205 BCE for the foundation of a temple to Honos and Virtus, presided over by the successful general's son; Ennius' *Ambracia* may have featured at the votive games held by Marcus Fulvius Nobilior, Ambracia's successful conqueror, in 186 BCE; and Pacuvius' *Paullus* could also have been performed at votive games after Pydna's conquest (though no games are recorded, Paullus himself, the subject of Pacuvius' play, was known for lavish *ludi*).[49] No information exists for the premier of Accius' *Brutus*, but we know it was restaged at the Apollonian Games (*Ludi Apollinares*) in 57 BCE and was slated for reperformance, again at the *Apollinares*, in 44 BCE. Balbus' *Iter* is reported to have been staged at special games hosted by Balbus himself in Gades, Spain, in 43 BCE. Two other possible *praetextae*, dealing with religious aetiologies, are said to have featured at the *Ludi Apollinares* and the *Ludi Megalenses* ('Great Games'), though their ascription to the genre is far from certain.[50]

If this practice of performing *praetextae* at *ludi* continued into the principate, then *Octavia* could have featured at the Plebian Games (*Ludi Plebeii*) honouring Galba's triumphant return to Rome in November 68 CE.[51] The games would have been a perfect occasion for Galba to justify his coup by reminding the Roman public of Nero's tyranny. The theatre would also have been the ideal venue for this reminder, not just because it involved a large, broad audience but also because of its intrinsic association with Nero. What better place to lay Nero's ghost to rest, and overcome his popular appeal, than in the theatre? Galba was certainly not averse to employing dramatic visual displays to criticize Nero's rule. His initial gesture of revolt involved standing on a tribunal, delivering a speech while surrounded by the death masks (*imagines*) of Nero's victims (Suetonius *Galba* 10.1). The spectacle was clearly intended to provoke outrage for the number of individuals condemned to death by Nero, while also preserving their memory and emphasizing their aristocratic status (for the death mask was an honour accorded only to patricians). Crucially, the effect and form of this display are like *Octavia*, which also represents Nero's victims – Seneca, Octavia, Poppaea, Agrippina – for the dual purpose of commemorating and arousing indignation at their fates. Performers in the play may even have worn masks representing the dead individuals' features (more on this below), prompting a yet closer association with aristocratic *imagines*. Unfortunately, there is too little evidence to confirm these possibilities, and Galba's parsimonious reversal of Nero's theatrical extravagances (Plutarch *Galba* 16) cautions against the idea that he expended much energy on *ludi*, but this remains a viable scenario for *Octavia*'s premiere.

If, however, we date *Octavia* to Vespasian's reign, it could have been performed at the games commemorating Vespasian's restoration of the Theatre of Marcellus. Having suffered damage during the civil conflict of 69 CE, perhaps corollary to the destruction of the Capitol, the Theatre of Marcellus was an apt venue for commemorating Rome's recently troubled past and the present renewal of peace. It was also a distinctly Julio-Claudian theatre, which would have paired well with *Octavia*'s contemplation of Julio-Claudian history. Suetonius reports that the *ludi* marking the theatre's restoration were lavish, and that on this occasion Vespasian 'recalled to the stage old entertainments as well' (*vetera quoque acroamata revocaverat*, *Vespasian* 19.1). Although the meaning of *acroamata* is unclear – musical performances or theatrical works? – it is possible that Suetonius refers to the reinstatement of more traditional dramatic genres, a category to which *Octavia* belongs.

The venue itself is no more certain than the occasion, though some inferences can be drawn from extant evidence. Public recitals under the principate ranged from small, invited gatherings (e.g. Pliny *Letters* 9.34) to large affairs convened in hired halls and presumably open to all comers (e.g. Juvenal *Satire* 7.82–7). The latter scenario seems more applicable to *Octavia* given the play's political significance and its positive portrayal of the Roman *populus*; if it was designed to counteract popular views of Nero, then it needed to reach a non-aristocratic audience. Such recitals were typically delivered by the author or by a hired speaker, which means that a single individual would have had to negotiate the multiple voices and characters intrinsic to drama.[52] They appear to have been noisy affairs, as well, with the audience voicing its views throughout. They must, in fact, have been quasi-dramatic, with speakers modulating their voices or gesturing to signify a change of character; on the spectrum from private reading to stage performance, the recital leans more towards the latter.

Alongside this culture of recitals, theatres continued to host performances of scripted drama under the principate,[53] and it is reasonable – though not irrefutable – to imagine *Octavia* being staged. The venue in this case was larger than the recital hall but similar in spatial arrangement. Roman theatres, unlike their Greek counterparts, were mostly enclosed spaces boasting a permanent backdrop (*scaenae frons*) several storeys high, decorated with statues and niches, and towering over the actors who would have stood on the raised stage in front. The raked auditorium (*cavea*) tended to be an independent structure, not built into a natural hillside in the Greek fashion. Awnings (*velaria*) stretched over the auditorium on hot days, to protect spectators from the sun, must have created a self-contained illusory space not unlike the interior of an eighteenth- or nineteenth-century opera- or playhouse. The grand style of these venues demanded an equally grand style of performance, a coloratura display to complement the impressively multistorey *scaenae frons*. Roman tragedy's increasing emphasis on visual and auditory spectacle – reported by Cicero (*Letters to Friends* 7.1) and confirmed by extant Senecan drama – would certainly have matched Rome's elaborate theatre buildings, though the precise relationship between these two aesthetic developments is unclear. Though less visually extravagant than Seneca's plays, *Octavia*, too, creates a sense of magnitude through affirmations of perpetual doom and disaster, and stylistically, through powerful monologues (e.g. Agrippina's ghost) and lyric laments (e.g. Octavia's opening) designed to showcase a performer's vocal skills and represent intense emotion. Additionally, the play's references to commemorative statuary (*Oct.* 609–12; 682–6; 795–9) complement the visual symbolism of the *scaenae frons* by creating a dialogue between the sculpted and theatrical embodiment of noble figures from Roman history. Whether or not *Octavia* was ever performed in a Roman theatre, its form and content certainly suit such a venue.

Other details of performance also rely on inferential reasoning. We may assume, for instance, that characters of senatorial rank in *Octavia* wore the purple-bordered toga for which the genre was named. But this play's *dramatis personae* are predominantly female and there is no extant information about female costuming in *praetextae*: the *stola* for Octavia and Poppaea, and slave garments for their nurses? Plausible, but uncertain. The style of masks is equally open to speculation, though evidence in this regard is more plentiful and suggestive. That actors in a *praetexta* wore masks seems assured: they did in all other Roman dramatic genres,[54] especially in tragedy, to which the *praetexta* is closely related. At the same time, though, *fabulae praetextae* pose a challenge to extant masking conventions because their characters are not the standard types encountered on the comic and tragic stage; they are specific historical individuals, whose roles do not always map onto the established tragic repertoire. While Accius' Tarquin or *Octavia*'s Nero could, conceivably, wear a tragic tyrant's mask, what about Accius' Brutus? Or Seneca in *Octavia*? Or the military heroes depicted by Naevius and Ennius?

No secure answer is forthcoming, but there is the enticing possibility that *praetexta* masks replicated specific individuals' features, in a manner resembling the death masks (*imagines*) owned by patrician families and paraded at aristocratic Roman funerals.[55] Association seems likely given that *praetextae* and *imagines* performed contiguous functions of commemoration and genealogical identification. There is also the tantalizing report from Suetonius (*Nero* 21.3) and Cassius Dio (63.9.5) that Nero, towards the end of his reign, sometimes performed in a mask representing his own face, or that of his deceased wife Poppaea. That Nero donned the likeness of a *deceased* person reinforces the probable connection between *imagines* and dramatic masks, while the overall activity, regardless of its eccentricity, furnishes a precedent for portraying actual historical personages in the theatre. The precedent is, moreover, directly relevant to *Octavia*: both Nero and Poppaea appear in this play and masks for them clearly existed in Nero's time.

Like any reconstruction of *Octavia*'s possible performance, the scenarios presented here involve a lot of guesswork. Most admit of no more than hypothetical formulation and must be treated with caution. Yet, intellectual precariousness aside, they are a useful exercise in attempting to understand *Octavia* as an event, not just a text. Even if *Octavia* was never staged in the ancient world – which seems improbable – it was nonetheless composed in accordance with prevailing dramatic conventions and conceived of as a theatrical work, which, for the playwright, must have encompassed knowledge of performance spaces, costumes, masks and acting styles – knowledge that eludes *Octavia*'s modern readership and consequently limits our appreciation of the work *as theatre*. Only by engaging in this imaginative speculation can we begin to restore *Octavia* to its rightful place on the Roman stage.

2

Historical Background

Octavia presupposes intricate knowledge of the imperial family and of the circumstances surrounding Nero's divorce. It contextualizes the dramatic present with repeated evocations of Julio-Claudian genealogy, which serve both to explain Octavia's predicament and to endow it with symbolic value by situating it within broader patterns of betrayal, intrigue and intergenerational murder. The play's version of events often resembles – in compressed form – the information found in Tacitus, and there is a good chance the author of the *Annals* used *Octavia* as a source.[1] This complicates the search for historical veracity and warns against the assumption that historiography provides a basis for evaluating *Octavia*'s fictionalization of history. Rather, *Octavia* itself becomes a quasi-historical document, its version of Nero's divorce integrated into the later historical record. Consequently, the ensuing discussion of divergence and overlap between *Octavia* and Tacitus is performed less with the aim of establishing 'what really happened' (to the extent that that can *ever* be established) than of enriching our understanding of *Octavia*'s historical vision: what it chooses to omit, include and adjust – and why.

2.1 Nero's divorce

Tacitus *Annals* 14.59–64 is the fullest extant account of Nero's divorce. The event marks a turning point in the narrative of Nero's crimes: with Burrus dead and Seneca in retirement, Nero is free to indulge his vicious impulses, first by ordering the executions of Faustus Cornelius

Sulla and Rubellius Plautus, distant claimants to the role of *princeps*, and then by accelerating preparations for his marriage to Poppaea Sabina. Octavia is put aside on a charge of sterility and Poppaea takes her place as Nero's wife. Upheaval ensues: Poppaea incites one of her servants to accuse Octavia of conducting an affair with a flute player; Octavia's handmaids are duly interrogated under torture, pain forcing some to admit the false accusations even though the majority stand firm. A civil divorce is issued and Octavia is removed to Campania, but the Roman populace protests so loudly against this action that Nero proposes to reinstate Octavia as his wife. The Roman public responds joyfully, overthrowing Poppaea's statues and setting up Octavia's in the forum and temples; an overzealous mob even tries to invade the palace but is violently repulsed. Then the situation is reversed once more: the mob is brought under control and Poppaea is reinstated. Her longstanding hatred of her rival is now amplified by fear; she convinces Nero that Octavia poses a threat to his rule, since the divorced daughter of Claudius is a prime candidate for marriage to a would-be usurper. Alarmed at this possibility, Nero summons Anicetus, the fleet commander involved in Agrippina's murder, and asks him to confess to adultery with Octavia, the reward being comfortable exile. Anicetus complies, and Nero issues an edict announcing that Octavia first seduced the commander and then acquired an abortion (he appears to have forgotten his recent charge of sterility). Octavia is sent to the island of Pandateria, where, a few days later, she receives the order for her death. Despite her protests of being 'only a sister' (*Annals* 14.64), not a wife, she is bound and her veins cut open, then, when this method fails to work, suffocated in a vapour bath. Her head is cut off and sent to Poppaea.

Tacitus' narrative exhibits multiple points of contact with the pseudo-Senecan *Octavia*, especially towards the episode's end, where Tacitus describes the sympathy onlookers feel for Octavia's plight. This focalization is a crucial feature, which, as Rolando Ferri remarks, interrupts the author's singular perspective and creates a scenario equivalent to *Octavia*'s final scene, in which the chorus regards and laments the heroine's fate.[2] Formal similarity is corroborated by content: some of Tacitus' nameless witnesses recall Tiberius' banishment of Agrippina the Elder and Claudius' of Julia Livilla, the first of whom is also recalled by the chorus at *Octavia* 932–40.[3] Both texts place Octavia in a catalogue of imperial women who meet violent deaths, parading them as paradigms of Octavia's present misfortune (*Oct.* 929–30). When the play's chorus implies that Octavia's fate is crueller than her predecessors' (*Oct.* 931), Tacitus responds by spelling out the comparison: these earlier victims of Julio-Claudian family politics were older women with happy memories to sustain them (*Ann.* 14.63); Octavia, by comparison, is pitifully young.

Tacitus continues with a vignette of Octavia's sufferings: her wedding day was a substitute for her funeral (*Ann.* 14.63); her new home contained nothing but grief (*Ann.* 14.63); her father was poisoned, and her brother shortly after (*erepto per venenum patre et statim fratre, Ann.* 14.63); finally, she endured the indignities of Nero's affair with Acte, being replaced by Poppaea and being accused of adultery (*Ann.* 14.63). Ferri argues convincingly that this portrait derives from *Octavia*: the heroine regards her marriage as a funeral (*Oct.* 23–4); stresses her constant sorrow (*Oct.* 70; 103–4); grieves 'bereft of her brother, her father snatched away through crime' (*per scelus rapto patre, / orbata fratre, Oct.* 103–4; the phrasing is similar to Tacitus', above); and resents Nero's affair with Acte (*Oct.* 105). Additionally, when Tacitus' Octavia refers to herself as 'no longer wife but sister only' (*iam viduam se et tantum sororem, Ann.* 14.64), she evokes a tradition that has roots not in historical reality – because Octavia had been adopted into another family to avoid the smear of incest in her marriage to Nero, and extant ancient records (inscriptions, edicts) omit any references to kinship – but in a motif from *Octavia*, for the play exploits the family relationship between Nero and Octavia as a parallel for Jupiter and Juno (*Oct.* 46–7; 219–20; 535; 789–90; 828).[4] The drama has Octavia remark, upon the event of Nero and Poppaea's marriage, 'I shall be Augustus' sister, not his wife' (*soror Augusti non uxor ero*, *Oct.* 658), a phrase that bears strong resemblance to Tacitus'. So, it seems indisputable that Tacitus borrows from *Octavia* in these final few chapters on the divorce. His borrowing, moreover, is a significant indication that Tacitus valued the play as an historical document, and that he expected at least some of his readers to grasp his evocations of the drama, implying that *Octavia* remained popular decades after its likely composition date.

Understandably, the play also takes liberties in its account of events, chiefly by telescoping Nero's divorce and remarriage into just three days when, in reality, they must have spanned more than a month. Historical calculations show that Plautus and Sulla were executed sometime between mid-April and mid-May 62 CE, when the senate learnt of their demise. Poppaea's pregnancy – barely glossed by Tacitus but flagged by *Octavia* (188; 591) as a motive for divorce must have begun in April 62, with the divorce put in motion shortly thereafter. Suetonius reports that only eleven days elapsed between the divorce's ratification and the marriage celebrations (*Nero* 35.3), which, given the restrictions of the Roman calendar, means that the wedding probably took place in the first week of June.[5] Octavia would have died on either 9 or 11 June, a few days after her removal to Pandateria.[6] The play, by contrast, encompasses the day before (*Oct.* 1–592), the day of (*Oct.* 593–689) and the day after the wedding (*Oct.* 690–982). Divorce is not mentioned in so few words, but the opening scene sees the nurse trying to convince Octavia to reconcile with her husband and produce heirs to strengthen the dynasty; a later scene has Seneca proposing an equivalent course for Nero (childlessness was clearly a problem for the couple, whether in the form of sterility, as alleged by Tacitus' Nero, or lack of conjugal relations, as *Octavia* maintains). This first part of the drama ends with Nero announcing the wedding for the following day.

Next, Agrippina's ghost appears in the early morning, just before dawn on the wedding day, and the ensuing nuptials are acknowledged obliquely in Octavia's exchange with the chorus. The day after the wedding sees a distraught Poppaea describing to her nurse the nightmare that visited her on her wedding night, followed by reports of popular revolt, Nero's harsh response and Octavia's exit into exile. Such compression obviously aids dramatic coherence, yet its purpose in the play is more than simply organizational. The three-day structure invites comparison between Octavia and Poppaea as prior and current wife, a parallel the playwright emphasizes through mirrored scenes: both women appear on stage in the company of a nurse, to whom they confess the contents of a terrible dream; both dreams involve Nero killing a family member; both nurses counsel forbearance and hope. The result is a sense of historical repetition, as Poppaea assumes not just Octavia's status but her fate as one of the emperor's female victims. Poppaea's marriage to Nero will likewise prove fatal, a future the playwright signals via this doubling of scenes and characters.[7] Structure *is* meaning in this play; it complements and elucidates the drama's view of historical reiteration.

Another of *Octavia*'s notable divergences from Tacitus is the presence of Seneca, who, in the latter narrative, has already retreated from the role of imperial advisor (*Ann.* 14.52–6). Granted Seneca remained an influential figure even after his departure from court in early 62 CE, but he was no longer actively involved in Neronian politics, and appears constantly to have sought greater solitude than Nero was willing to permit.[8] Dio's account (62.13.1), which has Burrus, praetorian prefect and Seneca's close ally, dissuading Nero from divorce in early 62, is unlikely to be correct.[9] The most plausible supposition is that Burrus had died before the matter of Nero's divorce was raised, and that Seneca, aware of his weakened position, hoped to escape Nero's autocratic capriciousness through self-imposed retirement. So why does *Octavia* present him in the active role of imperial advisor? Why this ahistorical inclusion?

The most likely explanation is *Octavia*'s pseudo-Senecan style. The play adopts Senecan motifs of cyclical evil,[10] draws upon Senecan passion-restraint scenes (especially between a nurse and a noblewoman) and models Nero on the archetypal Senecan tyrant, Atreus. Seneca's appearance in the play is one way of acknowledging this aesthetic debt. It also enables the playwright to formulate a complex interplay between tragic fiction and historical circumstance, by, for example, having Seneca's regretful return from exile (*Oct.* 377–84) resemble that of his own Thyestes (*Thy.* 411–14, 446–70) or making the Seneca–Nero confrontation (*Oct.* 437–589) equivalent to the minister and Atreus in *Thyestes* 176–335. This layering expresses not just literary influence, but a biographical/historical interpretation of Seneca's work; it assumes that the real Seneca lies somewhere behind the portrait of Thyestes, the real Nero behind Atreus, with Seneca's tragedy thereby treated as a quasi-historical source.[11] This overlap between Senecan tragedy and Neronian history will be examined more fully in the subsequent chapter ('Themes'). For now, it suffices to note that Seneca's mildly anachronistic presence in *Octavia* is key to the play's fusion of tragedy with history, as well as marking its main source of dramatic influence. It would seem strange, surely, to write a play in the Senecan tradition, about Nero, and *not* include Seneca himself!

Further, *Octavia* demonstrates its historical awareness by portraying Seneca and Nero's relationship as verging on dissolution. Seneca confesses that he was happier in exile, where his mind was 'free and sovereign' (*ubi liber animus et sui iuris mihi, Oct.* 383). This echoes the actual Seneca's praise of retirement from public life as the ultimate form of autonomy (*sui iuris* is a favourite Senecan phrase).[12] *Octavia* recalls Seneca's Corsican sojourn (381–2) to evoke his imminent departure from Nero's court. Further rifts appear in the ensuing encounter with Nero: the emperor asserts that he has outgrown Seneca's advice ('a soft old man should instruct boys', *praecipere mitem convenit pueris senem, Oct.* 445), while Seneca cautions that 'impetuous adolescence is more in need of guidance' (*regenda magis est fervida adolescentia, Oct.* 446). Frances Billot notes that this scenario is the reverse of Tacitus': *Octavia* has Nero all but dismissing Seneca while Seneca tries to maintain his advisory role; Tacitus, by contrast, has Seneca beg for retirement (*Ann.* 14.53–4), with Nero reluctant to let him go (14.55–6).[13] Nonetheless, both texts emphasize Seneca's dwindling influence – manifested in his losing an argument against his former pupil – and both depict Nero's hostility towards his former tutor. *Octavia*'s scene ends with Nero shouting at Seneca, 'Stop pressing the point! Enough. You're being obnoxious' (*desiste tandem, iam gravis nimium mihi, / instare, Oct.* 588–9) – an outburst that illustrates the emperor's impatience to assume moral autonomy and hints at the violence he could use to achieve it. This partnership is about to collapse.

It remains to consider two more differences between Tacitus and *Octavia*, one of which may be more apparent than real. The first is Octavia herself, whom Tacitus characterizes as fearful yet skilled at concealing her emotions. Confronted with the spectacle of Britannicus' poisoning, the Tacitean Octavia remains poker-faced: 'though young, she had learnt to hide grief, affection, every feeling' (*quamvis rudibus annis, dolorem caritatem, omnis adfectus abscondere didicerat, Ann.* 13.16). This seems, and has been remarked as,[14] the antithesis to the pseudo-Senecan Octavia, whom the nurse describes as 'unable to conceal her heavy grief, though compelled to do so by her cruel husband's anger' (*nec graves luctus valet / ira coacta tegere crudelis viri, Oct.* 47–8), and whose face, Nero claims, displays her hatred of him (*Oct.* 542). Yet the discrepancy is less pronounced than scholars think. True, tragedy demands some latitude of emotional expression, and a stony Octavia may not have been a successful protagonist.[15] But, notably, *Octavia*'s heroine grieves in secret, in her chambers, witnessed only by the nurse and the silent congregation of the play's audience. She remarks that fear prevents her from mourning the loss of her parents and from weeping for her brother's death (*Oct.* 65–7), which implies a scenario like Tacitus': Octavia cannot express her feelings openly for fear of reprisals. Mourning for Britannicus is tantamount to criticizing Nero; revenge would be swift and sure. The nurse makes this clear at 47–8: Nero's anger forces Octavia to veil her grief even though she struggles to do so. Hence, though they handle the issue differently, Tacitus and *Octavia* reach much the same conclusion: Nero's climate of fear compels those around him to cloak their responses by assuming a role.[16] The pseudo-Senecan and Tacitean Octavia are not so very different in this respect.

The final point of historical disparity between Tacitus and *Octavia* is the riot, which is jubilant in Tacitus and angry in the *praetexta*. Without further evidence, there is no knowing which account is correct, though Tacitus' seems more problematic because of narrative repetitions (Nero's separation from Octavia; her promised reinstatement; then separation again), which may indicate a muddling of divergent traditions in his sources.[17] Regardless of this difference, though, both the play and the annalist agree in having rioters topple Poppaea's statues (*Ann.* 14.61; *Oct.* 794–9) and storm the palace (*Ann.* 14.61; *Oct.* 801, 851–5). Tacitus' account suggests that the situation could easily erupt into violence: soldiers surround the palace to issue beatings and repel the mob at sword point (*Ann.* 14.61). The violence is given full rein in *Octavia*, with the crowd attempting to burn the palace and seize Poppaea (*Oct.* 851–5) and Nero responding with swift brutality (*Oct.* 846–61). In both texts, moreover, the riot is a catalyst for Octavia's condemnation, decided independently by Nero in the play and following Poppaea's persuasion in Tacitus. Once again, the two accounts converge in their evocation of the event's atmosphere despite discrepancies of detail.

Octavia's treatment of history is clearly valuable in its own right and should not automatically be subordinated to the record preserved in Tacitus, Suetonius and Dio. Granted a broadly accurate outline of events can be assembled from these historical texts and used to interrogate *Octavia*'s veracity, but any such enterprise must keep in mind *Octavia*'s own role in shaping that record. Fictionalization notwithstanding, *Octavia* demonstrates an acute grasp of historical motivation, and is especially adept at foreshadowing future events, whether through its dramaturgy or its persistent acknowledgement of historical repetition. History and drama work in tandem in this play, and the result is uniquely powerful.

2.2 Octavia and Nero's family

Octavia dwells obsessively on Nero and Octavia's Julio-Claudian lineage, not just as a source of lurid, tragic family history, but as a way of exploring the couple's competing claims to legitimacy. Parentage and genealogy are major themes in this play, doubtless reflecting actual, historical concerns about Nero's adoptive status and the tensions it produced in Claudius and Agrippina's family. The playwright's stance on the issue is unashamedly partisan: he condemns Nero as an inauthentic and champions Octavia as a genuine descendant with a direct, valid claim to *imperium*. The view is more ideological than rooted in genealogical fact, but careful navigation of extant historical records alongside a review of the tortuous Julio-Claudian family tree can help us appreciate the playwright's purpose.

The emperor Nero was born Lucius Domitius Ahenobarbus on 15 December 37 CE. He was the son of Agrippina the Younger and Gnaeus Domitius Ahenobarbus, a prominent patrician and Agrippina's first cousin once removed (Figure 1). Agrippina provided Nero with a direct genealogical link to Augustus through her own mother, Vipsania Agrippina, who was the daughter of Marcus Vipsanius Agrippa and Julia, Augustus' only child. Via both his parents, moreover, Nero could trace a line of descent from Augustus' sister, Octavia, whose marriage to Marc Antony produced two Antonias, the Elder (born 39 BCE) and the Younger (born 36 BCE). Antonia the Elder was Nero's paternal grandmother: she married Lucius Domitius Ahenobarbus and her son, Gnaeus, was Nero's father. Antonia the Younger, on the other side of Nero's family tree, was his great-grandmother: she married Nero Claudius Drusus – Livia's son and Tiberius' brother – to whom she bore Germanicus. Germanicus, in turn, fathered at least six children, including Agrippina the Younger, who – remarkably – survived the aftermath of her father's death[18] and was married to Gnaeus in 28 CE at the age of thirteen. The couple's only child, Nero, was born when Agrippina was twenty-two years old.

Nero's early life was turbulent, its circumstances dependent upon his mother's perilous path through the maze of Julio-Claudian politics.[19] In 39 CE, when Nero was not quite two, Agrippina was implicated in a plot against her brother, Caligula, and exiled to the Pontine islands.[20] Nero's father, Gnaeus, died near the end of 40 CE, and Nero was placed in the care of his aunt, Domitia. This year marked the lowest ebb in Agrippina's fortunes, but the situation soon changed when Caligula was assassinated in January 41, and his successor, Claudius, revoked Agrippina's sentence of exile as part of a general amnesty. She returned to Rome almost immediately and appears to have spent the next seven years cautiously building up a base of support among the senatorial aristocracy and members of Claudius' court. She remarried in 41, to Passienus Crispus, who died sometime in the mid-40s CE, leaving her with a substantial inheritance. Despite her dynastic prominence as Claudius' niece, Agrippina managed during this period not to fall foul of Claudius' wife Messalina, a feat that seems more remarkable when measured against the unprecedented number of aristocrats either exiled or executed in the first half of Claudius' reign, supposedly as a result of Messalina's paranoid ambitions.[21] Among Messalina's targets were Agrippina's sister, Julia

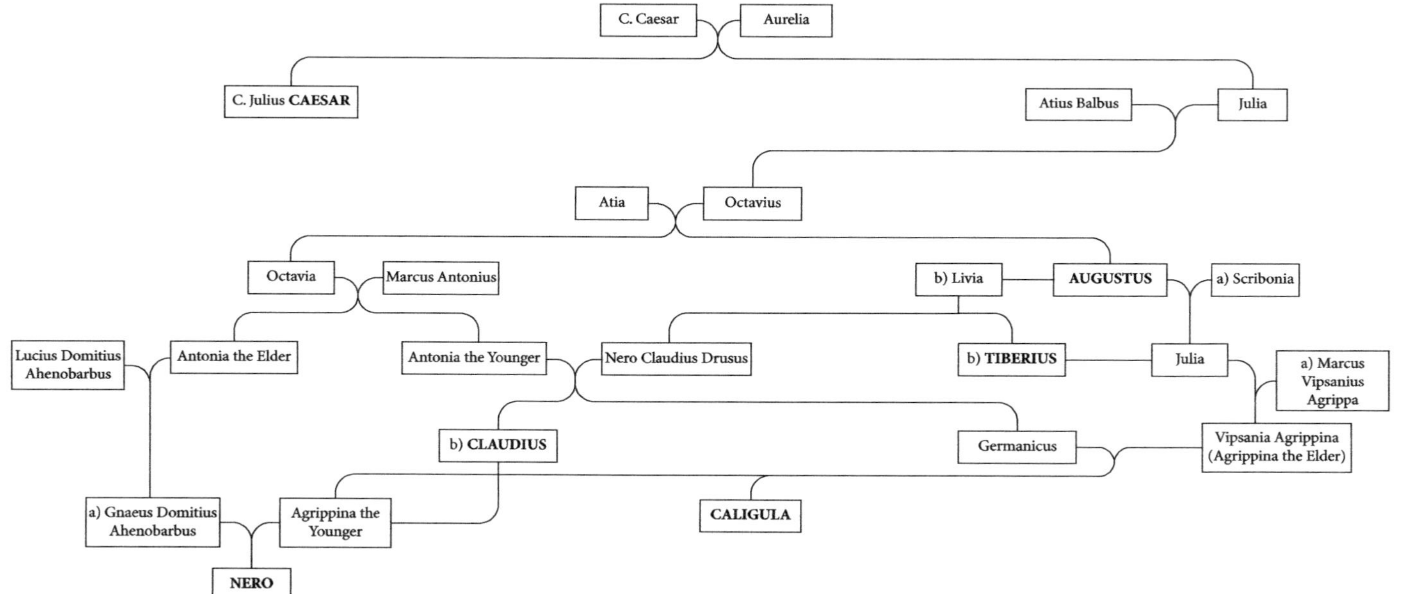

Figure 1 Nero's Family Tree.

Livilla, and the philosopher Seneca, one of Agrippina's closest allies: accused of having committed adultery together, Julia Livilla was exiled to Pandateria where she died in 41/2 CE, while Seneca was sent to Corsica, where he would remain in exile for eight years. Agrippina, however, survived the perils of association with Julia Livilla and Seneca, among others, and remained in Rome, becoming sufficiently influential and well-placed that when Messalina fell from power and lost her life in 48 CE, Agrippina succeeded in taking her position as Claudius' wife, empress and the most powerful woman in the empire.

Agrippina and Claudius were married in 49 CE, following senatorial legislation to allow a union between uncle and niece.[22] Shortly after, in early 50 CE, Claudius adopted Nero as his son. Agrippina's motives for pursuing this arrangement have been much distorted by hindsight and by a hostile historiographic tradition that cast her as a stereotypical 'wicked stepmother'.[23] While Nero's adoption into the *gens Claudia* enabled Agrippina to extend her power, as the mother of a potential future emperor, its most immediate justification was likely to have been more pragmatic: it strengthened the Julio-Claudian succession by providing the elderly Claudius with another heir in addition to his biological son, Britannicus, and it was a gesture of reconciliation for Rome's senatorial elite, whose hostile memories of Messalina had tainted Britannicus by association.[24] Claudius must have shared Agrippina's motives for adoption, even though it meant relegating his own child to second place: two heirs were better than one, and Nero symbolized the possibility of more harmonious relations between *princeps* and senate, while Britannicus stood as a reminder of Messalina's divisiveness and spectacular fall from grace. There is also the faint possibility that Britannicus was epileptic: his paternal uncle, Caligula, is said to have suffered from the condition (Suet. *Caligula* 50.2), and in Tacitus, epilepsy is the pretext Nero gives for Britannicus' seizures after the boy has been publicly poisoned (*Ann.* 13.16; see also Dio 60.33.10). Whilst the witnesses in Tacitus' narrative know this is a fabrication, it is not presented as implausible. Extant evidence permits nothing more than this light speculation, but if Britannicus was epileptic, then adopting a second, physically robust heir would also have been in Claudius' interests.

Pragmatics aside, Nero's adoption rapidly became a source of strain within the family as he began to be groomed for imperial succession. March 51 CE saw him nominated consul-designate and awarded the title 'leader of the youth' (*princeps iuventutis*), both of which honours had traditionally been used to mark potential successors.[25] In 53 CE, he was married to Octavia, Claudius and Messalina's daughter, a move that further intertwined the dynasty's Julian and Claudian strands, and by doing so, strengthened Nero's claims to power. But the move appears to have backfired at a personal level, with antagonism erupting between Claudius' biological and adopted sons. Britannicus is said to have continued calling Nero 'Ahenobarbus' (Tac. *Ann.* 12.41; Suet. *Ner.* 7.1), with Nero alleging Britannicus' illegitimacy in response (Suet. *Ner.* 7.1). Accusations of Nero being an imposter or interloper persisted throughout his time as emperor, too. Tacitus has Agrippina, alarmed at Nero's increasingly autocratic independence, call Britannicus 'the true and worthy heir of his father's power' and dismiss Nero as 'a grafted-on, adopted' member of the family (*Ann.* 13.14). Later still, long after Britannicus' assassination, Nero's critics would cite his biological lineage as shorthand for his inadequacies as emperor: the rebellious governor, Julius Vindex, is reported to have issued insulting edicts in which he referred to Nero as 'Ahenobarbus' (Suet. *Ner.* 41.1).

The historical veracity of these reports is hard to estimate. Jealous rivalry between Nero and Britannicus is not inconceivable, but we should be wary of positing personal motives at the root of political trends. The negative view of Nero as a fake heir supplanting the genuine Britannicus could just as easily have arisen retrospectively, once Nero had been demonized as a bad emperor. In the stark light of hindsight, Claudius' decision to promote his adopted son over his biological one must have seemed misguided in the extreme and there may have been a temptation to associate Britannicus' lineage with the lingering, unrealized possibility that he could have been a good ruler. In this schema, the adoptive brothers' bloodlines come to symbolize a choice between politically better and worse forms of imperial succession. Further, the slurs recorded in Tacitus and Suetonius are united in concentrating on Nero's patrilineal descent, which, besides activating memories of Domitius' tarnished reputation,[26] allows them to exaggerate Nero's separation from the Julio-Claudian *gens*.[27] In reality, of course, Nero claimed Julian heritage through both his mother and father, and a lesser but no less true connection to the Claudian *gens* via his grandfather, Germanicus. But his chief claims to the bloodline were matrilineal and in Rome's agnatic society, this may have been another reason for his representation as an outsider and usurper: his claims could never be as strong as Britannicus' dominantly patrilineal membership of the *gens Claudia*.

Octavia adopts a similarly hostile view of Nero's lineage. Octavia's nurse condemns Claudius for 'preferring someone else's seed to his own son' (*qui nato suo / praeferre potuit sanguine alieno satum*, *Oct.* 139–40), a decision she regards as the root of all the family's – and by extension, the empire's – present woes (143–73). Nero is characterized as a *hostis* (150), an outsider and public enemy[28] who infiltrates the Julio-Claudian household. Octavia echoes the nurse's antagonism, calling her husband 'a grafted Nero, son of Domitius' (*Nero insitivus, Domitio genitus patre*, 249), an insult that parallels those in Tacitus and Suetonius by citing Nero's patrilineal heritage. Her husband, Octavia maintains, is fundamentally a member of the Ahenobarbi – in character as well as birth – and fraudulently poses as a 'Nero', a name traditionally associated with the *gens Claudia*. Enjoyably for a play so attuned to issues of theatrical imitation, the Nero described in this line both is and is not himself: simultaneously a copy-cat Claudian and a genuine Domitius, both 'Nero' and Nero. The problem of his genealogy contributes to *Octavia*'s wider themes of real versus fake.

Octavia's statement is also striking for its use of proper names when the play overall tends to avoid them, and for the unusual adjective *insitivus*, 'grafted on', which deviates from the playwright's mostly pedestrian vocabulary. Tacitus' Agrippina employs similar terminology in angry reference to her son, *insitus ac adoptivus* ('grafted on and adopted' *Ann.* 13.14), and in Suetonius, Nero himself alleges that Britannicus is a 'suppositious' child (*subditivus*, Suet. *Ner.* 7.1). This cluster of similar vocabulary may suggest a common source; at the very least, it shows how *Octavia*'s narrative coheres with the dominant strands of Roman historiography/biography. Further evidence of coherence emerges from Nero's exchange with Seneca, when the *princeps* casts suspicion on Octavia's legitimacy because of Messalina's infidelities: 'her adulterous mother discredits her bloodline' (*incesta genetrix detrahit generi fidem, Oct.* 536). Though in this instance applied to Octavia rather than Britannicus, Nero's accusation serves the same function as in Suetonius (7.1, above), illustrating mutual antagonism between the adopted siblings, underscoring the value they place on their lineage and making Nero sound more than a little desperate to counteract derision of his adoptive status.

This theme of lineage penetrates even to the bedrock level of *Octavia*'s lexical choices. As Lauren Ginsberg observes, the playwright's frequent use of *ingens* ('enormous') functions as an etymological pun denoting actions 'within a *gens*' and 'against a *gens*'.[29] The word also hints at *innate* qualities, or propensities typical of a particular family group. Thus, when the chorus portrays Nero plotting *ingens nefas* ('enormous wickedness') against his mother (363), they point to the crime as intrafamilial, hostile to the family *and* characteristic of Nero.[30] In *Octavia*'s genealogically determined universe, such behaviour tends to be inherited. Appropriately enough, Agrippina likewise commits an *ingens scelus* ('enormous crime') by murdering Claudius to make way for Nero's rule (91). As one of the play's *leitmotifs*, *ingens* also has bearing on the theme of Nero's adoptive status, for it diagnoses his wickedness as a mark of his true bloodline.

In similar fashion, *Octavia* demonstrates a marked preference for terminology denoting biological relationships. Octavia twice refers to Britannicus as *germanus* (115; 182), which means a full brother, born from the same father and mother. Although elsewhere she uses the more common *frater* both for Britannicus (e.g. 62; 67) and Nero (e.g. 907), her purpose with *germanus* is to emphasize Nero's distance from, and intrusion upon, her Claudian family ties. The playwright also prefers to call Messalina a *genetrix* rather than a *mater* for related reasons: it draws attention to the blood connection from Messalina to Octavia as confirmation of the young woman's legitimate Claudian background.[31] In contrast to Nero's characterization as a Domitius, Octavia is called Claudia (671; 789; 803), Claudius' offspring (38; 278) and 'the glory of the Claudian family' (534), all of which stresses the genuineness of her bloodline and, consequently, her right to rule alongside Nero. Furthermore, of the six examples in the play, the title *Claudia/Claudia proles* is used most frequently by the chorus and by the messenger reporting the chorus' words; the playwright thereby implies popular belief in Octavia's legitimacy, placing her virtue, popularity and biological descent on the same continuum, just as he associates Nero's adoptive status with bad government and popular rebellion. Genealogy, in this play, is presented as a precondition of competent rulership.

In sum, *Octavia* constructs a simple polarity between Claudius' daughter at the centre of the Julio-Claudian family tree, and Nero at its edge. But the genealogical reality was far messier. Granted, Octavia's patrilineal lineage was predominantly Claudian: her father, Claudius, was the son of Nero Claudius Drusus and Antonia the Younger; Drusus, in turn, was Tiberius' brother and Livia's second son from her first marriage, to Tiberius Claudius Nero (died 33 BCE). Less often recognized, however, were the ties Octavia shared with her adoptive brother, the emperor Nero. For Octavia's mother, Valeria Messalina, was Nero's first cousin: Messalina's mother, Domitia Lepida, was the daughter of Lucius Domitius Ahenobarbus and Antonia the Elder, and Gnaeus Domitius Ahenobarbus' sister. Nero's grandparents were Octavia's great-grandparents, and this adoptive brother-and-sister pair were actually first cousins once removed (Figure 2). But *Octavia*'s playwright diligently avoids alluding to the heroine's genealogical links with the Ahenobarbi, instead painting a black-and-white picture of 'Domitius' versus 'Claudia'.

Another, crucial aspect of this contrast is how the playwright handles Nero and Octavia's adoptive sibling relationship, because before the pair could be married in 53 CE, Octavia had to be adopted into a different family, to avoid the appearance of incest (Dio 60.33.2). Contemporary inscriptions and coinage avoid mentioning any kinship relation between Octavia and Nero, instead referring to Octavia as Nero's wife.[32] But the play stresses her dual role as wife *and* sister, on the model of Juno's relationship to Jove. The nurse compares Octavia's sufferings to Juno's anguish at Jupiter's love affairs, and counsels calm obedience as the way to restore marital harmony (213–21). Seneca refers to Octavia as 'having been granted the lot of her brother's marriage bed, like Juno' (*sortita fratris more Iunonis toros*, 535). In a later scene, on the morning of Nero and Poppaea's wedding, Octavia declares that henceforth she will be 'Augustus' sister, not his wife' (*soror Augusti, non uxor ero*, 658). The formula recalls Juno in *Aeneid* 1.47 (*et soror et coniunx*) and Ovid's elaboration of the phrase in *Metamorphoses* 3.266 (*et soror et coniunx, certe soror*). Most likely it also alludes to Juno's angry outburst at the start of Seneca's *Hercules Furens*: 'sister of the thunderer – for this name alone is left to me' (*soror tonantis – hoc enim solum mihi / nomen relictum est*, 1–2).[33] Like Juno, Octavia is the abandoned wife to whom only the status of sister remains. This Olympian parallel heightens the significance of

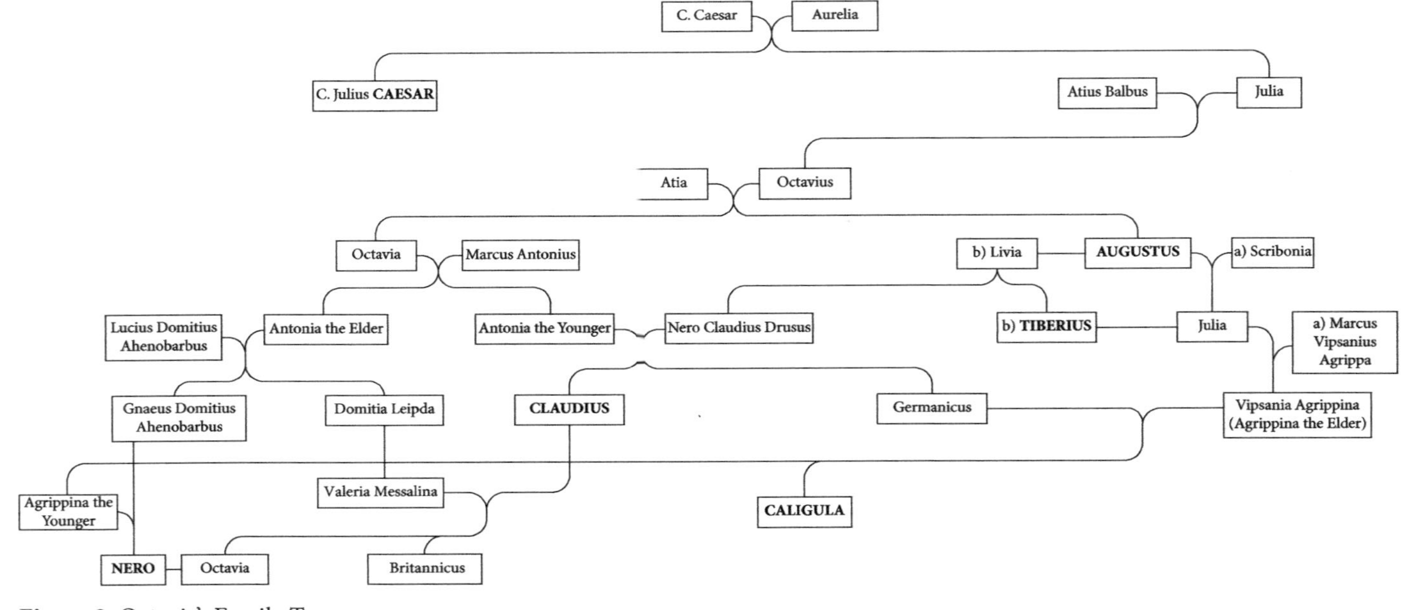

Figure 2 Octavia's Family Tree.

the play's events by imbuing them with mythic grandeur as well as seizing the opportunity to exploit Nero's ideological association with Jupiter.[34] The chief motive for its inclusion, however, is likely to have been genealogical, for emphasizing Octavia's sibling status allows the playwright to highlight her legitimacy, both as Claudius' daughter and as an all-powerful spouse, on the model of Juno.

Such notions of legitimacy reach their peak when the messenger characterizes Octavia's marriage to Nero as 'her rightful share in power' (*debitam partem imperi*, 790). Superficially, the implication is that Octavia acquires *imperium* through association with Nero, and that she is owed it as his lawful wife. But there is the deeper suggestion that *imperium* is Octavia's birth right, a suggestion confirmed by an anecdote in Cassius Dio (62.13.1–2), in which the praetorian prefect, Afranius Burrus, retorts that if Nero divorces Octavia, he should 'give her back her dowry (τὴν προῖκα)' by which – Dio glosses – he meant sovereignty (τὴν ἡγεμονίαν). The idea is that Octavia confers *imperium* on Nero rather than vice versa, as Claudius' lawful offspring and true heir to his power. Though neither the play nor Dio pursues the matter further, both evoke the scenario of Octavia ruling in her own right, a fanciful alternative history that excludes Nero, qua interloper, from the 'genuine' Julio-Claudian succession.

3

Themes

Rarely studied until the latter half of the twentieth century, *Octavia* is a rich text that affords ample interpretive material, much of which remains unacknowledged and under-exploited. After long years of being maligned as a second-rate Senecan spin-off, the play has increasingly become the subject of sophisticated scholarly treatment focused above all on its complex intertextuality, clever dramaturgy and politicized reading of history. This chapter tackles *Octavia*'s themes according to four broad categories: intertexts, repetition, the supernatural and commemoration. While it cannot aspire to comprehensive coverage, this selection of topics encompasses the play's most salient features and captures major trends in its scholarly analysis.

3.1 The poetic past

Octavia reads like a palimpsest of layered references to earlier literary texts. Its author evidently claimed strong knowledge of tragic drama, incorporating material from both Greek and Roman traditions. Nor is *Octavia*'s intertextuality restricted solely to theatrical genres: it draws extensively on Roman epic, which it weaves into broader narratives of civil conflict and imperial self-justification, and even ventures beyond the boundaries of poetry in its inventive use of Seneca's *On Clemency*. In fact, the play's engagement with Seneca is so substantial that it warrants separate treatment, hence the following subsections will cover Greek tragedy and Roman epic prior to a focused evaluation of *Octavia*'s Senecan qualities.

3.1.1 Greek tragedy

Octavia's most explicit and sustained engagement with Greek tragedy is its use of Sophocles' *Electra*.[1] As I note above in my discussion of *Octavia*'s genre, *Electra* functions as the dramatic and thematic touchstone for the first scene, where Octavia laments her parents' deaths on the model of the Sophoclean heroine. This model relies primarily on an analogy between Octavia's and Electra's domestic problems: the playwright likens Claudius to Agamemnon, killed by a scheming wife, and depicts Britannicus as a pitiable shadow of the avenging Orestes. Both Octavia and Electra dwell in oppressive households where they cannot adequately express their fears and where overt expressions of grief will be construed not just as personal outpourings but as criticism of those in power. In a move characteristic of 'belated' literary composition, the playwright makes Octavia's sufferings more extreme than Electra's, as though in a bid to exceed Sophoclean precedent and create a more comprehensively tragic scenario. Octavia complains that her troubles are incomparable:

> O mea nullis aequanda malis
> fortuna, licet
> repetam luctus, Electra, tuos:
> tibi maerenti caesum licuit
> flere parentem,
> scelus ulcisci uindice fratre,
> tua quem pietas hosti rapuit
> texitque fides.
> me crudeli sorte parentes
> raptos prohibet lugere timor
> fratrisque necem deflere uetat,
> in quo fuerat spes una mihi
> totque malorum breue solamen.

> O my misfortune, unrivalled
> by any evils, although

I repeat your grief, Electra:
you were allowed to weep, sorrowful
    for a murdered parent,
to punish the crime with your avenging brother
whom you dutifully saved from the enemy
    and loyally hid.
Fear prevents me from lamenting
parents snatched by cruel fate
forbids me from crying for my dead brother,
who was my only hope
and brief solace in so many troubles.

Oct. 57–69

The passage is a self-conscious acknowledgement of Octavia's (and thus, *Octavia*'s) literary antecedents. Just as the heroine reprises Electra's lament, so the playwright resurrects and recasts Sophoclean material. Octavia surpasses Electra in having endured the death of both parents rather than just one, and in no longer having a brother to help avenge her father's murder. Whereas Orestes' absence ensured his safety, Britannicus' is absolute and irreversible. There may be a deeper evocation of Sophocles' *Electra* here as well, because in that tragedy Orestes manufactures a report of his own death as a subterfuge when returning to Argos, and the reunion scene between Electra and her brother begins with the former believing and grieving that the latter has died. Like Octavia, Electra regrets her brother's death as the loss of her only remaining hope (αἵ μοι μόναι παρῆσαν ἐλπίδων ἔτι, Soph. *El.* 810, cf. *Oct.* 68 *in quo fuerat spes una mihi*) and uses an earlier mythological precedent – of Amphiaraus and Alcmaeon – to compare a son's successful vengeance with her own unhappy bereavement (*El.* 837–48). Just as Octavia declares her circumstances grimmer than Electra's, so Sophocles' Electra declares hers grimmer than Alcmaeon's, and in both cases the problem is a brother's death, which thwarts the heroines' desire for retribution. In Electra's case, of course, this death turns out to be a mirage, while in Octavia's it is real. The result for Octavia is a more immutable tragedy, in which a dismal ending seems unavoidable, as opposed to Electra's happy reversal of fortune in which Orestes returns to kill Clytemnestra and Aegisthus. Thus, *Octavia*'s allusions to Sophocles' *Electra* invite audiences to expand the heroines' immediate similarities into a broader comparison of their respective fates. Besides evoking the playwright's competitive relationship with a tragic predecessor, and the drama's aspiration to exceed or 'cap' prior instantiations of tragedy, these allusions also inform Octavia's representation as a tragic protagonist and shape the audience's response to her misfortune.

More broadly, *Octavia*'s playwright displays a preference for invoking Greek tragic paradigms in the heroine's extended lyric scenes, which occupy the drama's beginning and end. While the intertext of Sophocles' *Electra* structures the opening scene, Octavia's final exchange with the chorus (899–982) is reminiscent of Sophocles' *Antigone*: both protagonists are victims of angry tyrants; both are brought onto stage under guard and led away to their deaths; and both are accompanied by a sympathetic chorus that attempts consolation by enumerating prior examples of prominent individuals meeting their doom.[2] The parallels are chiefly structural rather than lexical, but their cumulative effect makes *Antigone*'s presence indisputable. Further, the consolatory chorus at *Octavia* 924–57 provides particularly close echoes of *Antigone* 944–87, because both passages cite a mixture of positive and negative paradigms. *Antigone*'s chorus sings of Danae's unjust imprisonment (944–54); followed by Lycurgus' deserved incarceration for his attempted banning of Bacchic rites (955–65); followed by the sufferings of Cleopatra and Phineus' children (966–87); the uniting theme is that pain and imprisonment can be inflicted even on those of royal background. *Octavia*'s chorus concentrates exclusively on examples of women from the protagonist's family: Agrippina the Elder, wife of Germanicus, exiled unfairly by Tiberius after her husband's death (932–40); Livilla, Germanicus' sister, tried and executed for poisoning her second husband, Tiberius' son Drusus (941–3); Julia Livia, Livilla's daughter, falsely charged with incest and immorality by Messalina and dying either by execution or by her own hand (944–6); Messalina (947–51) and finally, Agrippina the Younger, murdered by Nero (952–57). Livilla's inclusion in this list of otherwise undeserved punishments is puzzling, and the best explanation is that *Octavia*'s playwright had *Antigone* 944–87 in mind: both choruses commence with an example of unwarranted suffering followed by an example of merited penalty. Rolando Ferri notes a further connection between the opening examples of Danae and Agrippina the Elder, who are imprisoned despite their royal standing and their having given birth to royal offspring.[3]

Beyond these specific evocations of *Antigone*, it is also clear that *Octavia*'s choruses employ historical *exempla* on the model of mythic paradigms in Greek tragic choruses. History in *Octavia* resembles myth in its ready supply of conspicuous individuals and narrative patterns to measure oneself against, and in its clustering of these patterns around particular family groups. In this regard, *Octavia*'s vision of prolonged and repetitious Julio-Claudian misery resembles the Theban cycle, or the intergenerational crimes of the Tantalid house. The *praetexta*'s citation of tragic material serves to enhance Octavia's prestige and the significance of her suffering: she is not just Nero's young, downtrodden, soon-to-be ex-wife, but a tragic heroine of Antigone's and Electra's stature, and someone whose divorce and death signals the end of Julio-Claudian rule.

As an epilogue to these tragic intertexts, *Octavia*'s final chorus compares Octavia to Iphigenia, first wishing she could be saved like Iphigenia at Aulis (*Oct.* 972–8), then declaring Rome more barbarous than Tauris (978–81). Though neither is a direct allusion to Euripides,[4] and both could instead be taken as generic citations of myth, nonetheless these references fit within *Octavia*'s persistent use of Greek tragic models for its protagonist. Like Sophocles' *Electra*, *Iphigenia in Aulis* evokes the happy resolution Octavia cannot achieve. Both Octavia and Iphigenia are young, virginal women[5] whose death is a catalyst for conflict. Both are sacrificed – more and less literally – to another woman's cause: Nero executes Octavia in order to possess Poppaea while Agamemnon has his daughter ritually killed in order to recover Helen.[6] Each faces death because of her father's weakness, a parallel reinforced by *Octavia*'s repeated analogies between Claudius and Agamemnon. But the chorus' hope for gentle breezes to convey Octavia far from her bitter suffering (976–7) has already been foreclosed by history. As happens with the play's earlier references to Sophocles' *Electra*, this mythological comparison heightens the harshness of historical reality: here is a world where brothers never return from presumed oblivion and no deities intervene to save the innocent.

Citation of the Iphigenia myth also signals *Octavia*'s generic affiliations to tragedy, with the same consequence of emphasizing the present drama's bleakness in comparison to its Greek tragic counterparts. Ending on a grimmer note than either *Iphigenia in Aulis* or *Iphigenia in Tauris*, *Octavia* evokes this material competitively, to advertise its story as more fully, fundamentally tragic than its models. Thus, the chorus' reference to Tauris may be taken as conveying the impossibility of family reunion, with Iphigenia's recovery of Orestes becoming a foil for Octavia's irrevocable loss of Britannicus.[7] The reference can also be read with Octavia in the victim's role, as a sacrifice for which Rome has no excuse, and which exceeds in barbarity the Taurian habit of sacrificing strangers; Octavia's death is presumed more heinous for its having been inflicted by her own people. The final image of Rome rejoicing in citizen bloodshed (982) illustrates once again how the brutal realities of history outweigh even the darkest parts of myth.

Overall, then, Greek tragic intertexts in *Octavia* perform the double – and contradictory – function first of elevating and universalizing the sordid tale of Nero's divorce, as though it, too, could claim the endurance and cultural vitality of myth, and second of highlighting the singular, obdurate reality of Octavia's suffering, which admits of no divine intervention or reversal of fortune. Roman history acquires a tragic colouring in *Octavia* not just in recognition of the play's proximity to tragedy, but in affirmation of the historical episode's greatness and general applicability: Nero and Octavia's story becomes a paradigm on the level of Electra's, Antigone's and Iphigenia's. At the same time, these paradigms are acknowledged as falling short: they cannot fully encapsulate Octavia's experience, and their very limitation is likewise an expression of tragic sentiment. Comparison with mythic heroines makes Octavia's fate seem all the sadder.

3.1.2 Roman epic

Accompanying *Octavia*'s Greek tragic intertexts is its pervasive and equally vital appropriation of Roman epic. The stanza that begins with Octavia apostrophizing Electra (57–64) ends with an allusion to Lucan's *Civil War*, a transition that testifies not only to the play's intertextual richness, but also to its coupling of domestic tragedy with national catastrophe, of private, Julio-Claudian strife with the ever-present threat of internecine conflict. Bemoaning the deaths of mother, father and brother, Octavia concludes, 'now, preserved only for grief, I remain the shadow of a great name' (*nunc in luctus servata meos / magni resto nominis umbra*, 70–1). The source text is Lucan's famous comparison of Pompey and Caesar in Book 1 of his *Civil War*: Caesar is the lightning bolt, unflagging in his destructive ambition, and already famed for his military skill, while Pompey is the old oak, respected yet tottering, vulnerable and supported only by his past glories (1.129–57). Lucan's Pompey 'stands, the shadow of a great name / of the name *Magnus*' (*stat magni nominis umbra*, 1.135).[8]

He is simultaneously a relic of his former reputation and of his former self.

Octavia's citation of this line achieves complex effects. At the simplest level, Octavia reflects Pompey's immobility (*stat*; *resto*), which prefigures her as an impediment to Nero's tyrannous designs.[9] Like Lucan's Pompey, Octavia is largely passive, doomed from the outset, yet also a figurehead of popular, anti-autocratic sentiment. Just as Pompey enjoys the Roman people's adulation (e.g. *Civil War* 1.131–3; 7.10–14), so Octavia receives their unsolicited *favor* (183; 648; 792; 877).[10] This parallel imbues *Octavia*'s domestic scenario with momentous political consequences, as though, like the civil war between Julius Caesar and Pompey, Nero's dismissal of his former wife represented a hinge point in Roman history, a conflict that signalled the defeat of republican ideals and the triumph of tyranny.[11] The Nero of this *praetexta* plays Julius Caesar to Octavia's Pompey,[12] his role encompassing the reckless, aggressive selfishness that characterizes Lucan's anti-hero and, by extension, the political system he comes to represent. Although Nero's frustrations in *Octavia* are chiefly marital, his attitudes towards political and personal setbacks occupy the same continuum: his treatment of Octavia is congruent with his belligerent disrespect for the Roman state. Thus, when Octavia quotes Lucan, she underscores her self-identification as a victim not just of *a* Caesar, but of Caesarism overall, that totalizing drive for power that never baulks at bloodshed. Her allusion to *Civil War* may further remind *Octavia*'s audience that Lucan himself was another Neronian victim.[13]

This political partisanship blends into themes of commemoration. Besides evoking Roman civil conflict, and the wider context of republican versus Caesarean government, Octavia's *magni nominis umbra* also evokes her perilous position on the losing side of history and her consequent risk of erasure from collective memory. It intimates her own ghostlike status (*umbra*) as a faint reflection of her former self and, more literally, as a deceased historical personage whom Nero has forcibly removed from the Julio-Claudian narrative. The allusion may even signal Octavia's concern for the waning prestige of the Claudian name (if we follow Anthony Boyle in interpreting its *magnum nomen* as 'Claudius').[14] The overall effect is an impression of impending finality: the marriage will end, as will Octavia's life and the Julio-Claudian dynasty. From the play's historical perspective, all these events already occupy the shadowy land of the past. But they also need to be remembered, which is the final, most powerful purpose of this Lucanian intertext: it pursues Lucan's programme of celebrating the defeated and resisting their consignment to oblivion. Octavia, like Lucan's Pompey, is granted her rightful place in history; she will remain in the collective memory despite marginalization then murder by Nero. Her affirmation of 'remaining' (*resto*) evokes endurance, not just finality; she will not be forgotten even as a shade.

This example is representative of *Octavia*'s intricate engagement with Roman epic, references to which punctuate the rest of the play, united in their evocation of civil war and the failures of Julio-Claudian government. Like the *praetexta*'s use of Greek tragedy these allusions are concentrated in specific scenes, notably the exchange between Nero and Seneca at 377–592. The first part of this confrontation focuses on Augustus as a guiding paradigm for Nero's rule. Seneca adopts a Vergilian tone to praise Augustan peace and clemency, while Nero undercuts him with recollections of the *princeps*' earlier participation in civil war. The debate is framed as a contest between the *Aeneid*'s political optimism and the brutal *realpolitik* of Lucan's *Civil War*. The first, albeit attenuated, allusion to Roman epic appears in Seneca's opening monologue about the myth of Ages, where the most debased race of men is described as having 'invaded its parent's innards' (*<u>in parentis viscera</u> intravit suae*, 416) in distant echo of Anchises' plea to Caesar and Pompey in the underworld (*Aeneid* 6.833): 'don't turn your mighty strength against the fatherland's innards' (*neu <u>patriae</u> validas <u>in</u>*

viscera *vertite viris*).[15] In *Octavia*, the intertext functions as a warning, not just of the need to avoid civil conflict, but of that conflict's imminence; this is an era ripe for internecine strife.

Fuller appropriation of the *Aeneid* follows, as Seneca urges Nero to 'spare the downtrodden' (*parcere afflictis*, 473) in likely evocation of Anchises' famous *parcere subiectis* ('spare the conquered' *Aen.* 6.853).[16] In echoing the line, *Octavia* casts Seneca as a father figure delivering a lesson in Roman government to Nero qua son. It also makes the *Aeneid* a yardstick of the ideal principate, as though Vergil's epic were less a fictional creation than a socio-political pamphlet. Seneca continues in this vein when, in the following section of his speech, he models young Augustus' tribulations on those of Aeneas:

> illum tamen Fortuna iactavit diu
> terra marique per graves belli vices,
> hostes parentis donec oppressit sui.
>
> But Fortune tossed him about for a long time
> on land and sea, through war's harsh vicissitudes,
> until he crushed his father's enemies.
>
> *Oct.* 479–81

The passage's similarity to the *Aeneid*'s prologue has been well observed: Aeneas is likewise 'tossed about greatly on land and sea' (*multum ille et terris iactatus et alto*, *Aen.* 1.3) and 'suffers greatly in war' (*multa quoque et bello passus*, *Aen.* 1.5) before founding a city and bringing his household gods to Latium (*Aen.* 1.5–6).[17] Both passages present a hero emerging triumphantly from misfortune, and both employ a temporal clause (*dum*, *Aen.* 1.5; *donec*, *Oct.* 481) to convey a sense of purposive momentum and closure. But the really striking aspect of this allusion is its conflation of Aeneas with Augustus, which amounts to a blatant historicizing of the *Aeneid*. Rather than accept Vergil's oblique and cautious association of Aeneas with Rome's first *princeps*, *Octavia*'s author portrays the former as a transparent version of the latter. As we shall see, this is not the only time *Octavia* treats a work of fiction as an historical document, but the immediate purpose of this Augustus–Aeneas conflation is to epitomize Seneca the character's hopeful vision of *pax* and *princeps*. Seneca alludes to the *Aeneid* to justify Augustus' participation in civil conflict, first by portraying his wars as necessary, political retribution (the wording of *Octavia* 481 seems reminiscent of the *Res Gestae* in this regard),[18] and second, by linking them to the forward-looking, optimistic momentum of the *Aeneid*'s proem.[19] Seneca in *Octavia* approaches the *Aeneid* as a work of unabashed Augustan propaganda and an instruction manual for Nero to rule successfully.

Nero's response flips this vision. In place of clemency and diplomacy, he affirms the bloodied ruthlessness of Augustus' rise to power. His account of Octavian and Antony's proscriptions (503–13) draws on the standard civil war *topoi* found in Livy, Seneca the Elder (*Suasoria* 6) and, most importantly, Lucan's *Civil War*: severed heads mounted on the *rostra*, decaying and dripping gore; sorrowful senators gazing upon them but not being permitted to weep or grieve for family members.[20] The images recall the Sullan proscriptions in Book 2 of Lucan, where severed heads are carried through the city before being piled in the forum (*Civil War* 2.160–1) and relatives struggle to recognize the mutilated remains (*Civil War* 2. 166–8).[21] The accompanying interdiction of mourning – *flere nec licuit suos* ('nor were they allowed to weep for their kin', *Oct.* 511) may also allude to *Civil War* 2.38–42, in which a distraught mother, anticipating the coming disaster of Caesar's invasion, tells her companions that they have the freedom to weep now (*nunc flere potestas*, 2.40), while fate hangs in the balance and before the tyranny of one-man rule stifles mourning as a sign of opposition. Octavia admits an equivalent prohibition at 65–7: grief must be repressed for fear of autocratic retaliation.

Nero rounds out his evocation of Lucan's *Civil War* by recalling one of its most famous lines: conflict at Philippi and Naulochus leaves the world 'shaken by the great strength of its leaders' (*concussus orbis viribus magnis ducum*, *Oct.* 518), a clear echo of *Civil War* 1.5, in which Caesar and Pompey's war 'is waged with all the forces of a shaken world' (*certatum totis concussi viribus orbis*). The implication, here and throughout Nero's speech, is that Augustus bears closer resemblance to Lucan's Caesar than to Vergil's Aeneas. In place of Seneca's positive assessment, Nero depicts Augustus as an unscrupulous, power-hungry autocrat. Nor is this just a clash of political views. Rather, *Octavia*'s appropriation of Vergilian and Lucanian epic highlights the role of those literary works in constructing imperial identity and promulgating a partisan image of the principate: Seneca uses Vergil to evoke a merciful, peaceful, dutiful Augustan regime following a brief (but necessary) period of bloodshed; Nero uses Lucan to affirm the ongoing oppression and violence at the heart of the imperial project, in blatant justification of his own brutality.[22]

Following this scene, the play's remaining allusions to Roman epic return the focus to Octavia. The titular heroine compares herself to Aeneas when, on the morning of Nero and Poppaea's marriage, she assures the chorus, 'I have endured worse. This day will grant an end to my distress, if only through death' (*graviora tuli. / dabit hic nostris finem curis vel morte dies*, *Oct.* 652–3). Her words echo Aeneas' as he comforts his despairing companions, shipwrecked on the shores of Carthage: 'oh you who have suffered worse, god will grant an end to these things as well' (*o passi graviora, dabit deus his quoque finem*, *Aen.* 1.199).[23] Like her earlier association with Lucan's Pompey, Octavia here is cast in the role of a sympathetic leader who commands the respect of her subjects. Yet there is also a darker side to this comparison because Octavia, unlike Vergil's Aeneas, foresees no divinely ordained end to suffering; only death, not a benevolent god, will free her from her troubles.

Octavia's final evocation of Roman epic is disputed and requires some explanation. The manuscript tradition has her say to the chorus, 'let the ship's helmsman at last seek the shores of the Pharian land' (*petat puppis rector / tandem Phariae litora terrae*, *Oct.* 970–1), which implies that she is destined for Egypt. But Justus Lipsius emended *tandem Phariae* to *Pandatariae* in the sixteenth century, chiefly on the basis that Tacitus' *Annals* 14.63 gives Pandateria as Octavia's place of exile. There is little to recommend Lipsius' emendation: it is unmetrical (*Pandatāriae* instead of *Phăriae*); it is largely unnecessary given that the manuscript reading is not corrupt; and it makes the mistake of subordinating *Octavia*'s 'fictional' portrayal to Tacitus' 'factual' one (a problem I flagged in Chapters 1 and 2). Despite these concerns, the emendation has been adopted by many modern editions[24] in what Anthony Boyle refers to as 'A triumph of consensus history over textual transmission and prosody of staggering dimensions.'[25] Retaining *Phariae* is a better choice,[26] not just for reasons of scansion but because it coheres with Nero's earlier order that Octavia be removed 'far away, to a remote shore' (*procul in remotum litus*, *Oct.* 875) – Pandateria, by contrast, was too near Italy to qualify as a truly *remotum litus*.[27]

Reading *Phariae* at *Octavia* 971 also complements the play's thematic association of Octavia with Lucan's Pompey. The heroine begins the drama by evoking Pompey's obsolescence (*Oct.* 71) and ends with a reference to Egypt's shoreline, where Lucan's Pompey arrives seeking refuge only to be betrayed and killed in the aftermath of Pharsalus. Read in this way, Octavia's last words perform an act of ring composition and anticipate the sad end not only of her life but of the anti-tyrannical sentiment she has come to represent. Egypt spells her doom, just as it does for Pompey. Though such interpretation must remain tentative given the lines' disputed content, this kind of final disquieting reference to Lucan suits the play's engagement with Roman epic and especially with Roman epic's visions of Roman history.

3.1.3 Seneca

Octavia engages more deeply and pervasively with Seneca than with any other author. As the leading intellectual of the Neronian era, himself a tragic playwright as well as philosopher and statesman, Seneca was unsurprisingly the greatest source of inspiration for a drama about Nero.[28] *Octavia* draws upon the entire spectrum of his work, from *Medea* to *Natural Questions*,[29] but concentrates above all on two closely related texts, *Thyestes* and *On Clemency*, which it employs to devastating effect. Once again, the bulk of these allusions feature in the Seneca–Nero dialogue, which not only represents a clash between Vergilian and Lucanian worldviews, but also reimagines the minister's ineffectual attempts to restrain Atreus in Act 2 of Seneca's *Thyestes*. The arc of the exchange, alongside the interlocutors' personal qualities, demonstrates a clear debt to Seneca's tragedy: an advisor tries to persuade a headstrong tyrant towards a more moral course of action, but his warnings founder in the face of brute autocratic confidence. *Octavia*'s Nero embodies Atreus in his desire for vengeance against kin (*Oct.* 463; *Thy.* 176–8), disregard for popular sentiment (*Oct.* 454–61 and 572–9; *Thy* 204–18), preference for ruling through force and fear (*Oct.* 457–61 and 492–4; *Thy.* 205–12 and 247–8), assumed superiority to the gods (*Oct.* 449; *Thy.* 885–8) and delight in the exercise of power for its own sake (*Oct.* 451–3; *Thy.* 218).[30] He is a clever speaker, adept at parrying his minister's recommendations by reiterating and redefining their key concepts: in response to Seneca's Stoic plea for 'appropriate' conduct (*quod decet*, 454), Nero declares it 'appropriate for Caesar to be feared' (*decet timeri Caesarem*, 457); he puns on 'clemency' (*clementia*, 442) as 'madness' (*dementia*, 496) and boasts of Rome's enslavement (*servit*. . . / *Roma*, 492–3) when Seneca urges the state's preservation (*ut serves*, 490). *Octavia*'s Seneca, for his part, resembles *Thyestes*' minister, advising his monarch to value justice and honour above personal fulfilment and not to underestimate the consequences of hostile public opinion. The only difference is that *Octavia*'s Seneca, unlike the minister, never ends up complying with the tyrant's viewpoint.

Verbal echoes reinforce these thematic similarities. Nero, like Seneca's Atreus, feels indignant at the prospect of remaining 'unavenged' (*inultus*, 463; cf. *Thy.* 178) and declares it 'spineless' not to know the extent of one's power (*inertis*, 453; cf. *Thy.* 176). He misuses the Stoic concept of *fortuna* (451) in the same way that Atreus warps the philosophical ideal of the 'greatest good' (*maximum . . . bonum*, *Thy.* 205). His need to inspire dread in his subjects likewise evokes Seneca's Atreus, but via the more complex method of alluding to Seneca's chief model: Accius' Atreus. The Accian tyrant's most famous line – 'let them hate so long as they fear' (*oderint dum metuant Atr.* 203–4 *TRF*²) – was a favourite of Seneca's, who quoted it frequently in his prose (*On Clemency* 1.12.4, 2.2.2; *On Anger* 1.20.4) and refashioned it for *his* Atreus as the equally quotable 'let them want what they don't want' (*quod nolunt velint*, *Thy.* 212).[31] *Octavia*, too, reworks this Accian tag, first by having Nero declare, 'Caesar should be feared' (*decet timeri Caesarem*, 457), and then, a line later, 'they must fear me' (*metuant necesse est*, 458). While neither line captures the pithiness of Accius and Seneca, context confirms the allusion, as does the subjunctive *metuant*. Nero in *Octavia* belongs to a long Roman tradition of depicting Atreus as the archetypal tyrant, and of associating him with actual, historical autocrats.[32]

This blend of history and fiction is yet another example of *Octavia*'s author interpreting literature in historical terms. The playwright clearly perceives Seneca's *Thyestes* as a thinly veiled comment on the Neronian court; s/he detects Nero behind Seneca's Atreus and Seneca himself behind the minister.[33] It is an apt approach for an author of historical fiction and may even indicate her/his interpretive preferences given *Octavia*'s equivalent conflation of Aeneas and Augustus (479–81, above). By modelling the Nero–Seneca exchange on that of Atreus and his minister, *Octavia* treats Seneca's *Thyestes* as an anxious reflection of Seneca's own situation: the struggling advisor who can no longer control his assertive, all-powerful pupil.

Besides associating Seneca with *Thyestes*' minister, *Octavia* also associates him with the character of Thyestes. Both figures regret returning from exile: Thyestes recalls that his life in the woods was safe and happy, free from the fears that attend great power (*Thy.* 446–70), while Seneca in *Octavia* confesses that he was happier in Corsica where he enjoyed greater autonomy and was likewise free from fear (*Oct.* 377–84). Once again, the association appears to derive from a historicizing interpretation of Senecan tragedy, in which Thyestes' return from exile to the perilous seductions of wealth and rulership represent Seneca's own move from the margins to the very peak of Roman government, with all its accompanying anxieties.

Bolstering this imaginative reconstruction of the historical Seneca is *Octavia*'s equally creative deployment of Seneca's philosophical treatise, *On Clemency*, which the philosopher wrote for Nero in 56 CE. The text's presence in *Octavia* has long been recognized, with Friedrick Bruckner providing the fullest list of parallels.[34] Its influence is initially signalled at 442, where Seneca declares, 'clemency is a great cure for fear' (*magnum timoris remedium clementia est*) and proceeds to remind Nero that the gods will judge his deeds (448), a claim that evokes the real Seneca's advice at *Clem.* 1.7.1–2. Ensuing discussion of what 'befits' a ruler (*decet*, *Oct.* 454–7) recalls Seneca's definition of *clementia* as a virtue most fitting (*decet*) for kings and emperors (*Clem.* 1.3.3), while the speakers' disagreement over whether Nero should restrain his power (*quod licet*, *Oct.* 453–4) corresponds to *On Clemency*'s warnings about the 'licence of self-destruction' (*pereundi licentia*, *Clem.* 1.1.8). The perils of ruling through fear and coercion are major themes at *Octavia* 457–61 and *On Clemency* 1.12.4 and 1.19.5, and when *Octavia*'s Nero protests the moral demands restricting his behaviour – 'am I alone forbidden to do what everyone is allowed?' (*prohibebor unus facere quod cunctis licet?* 574) – he echoes the main idea of *On Clemency* 1.8.1, where the general populace is accorded freedoms denied to emperors, and Nero utters an imagined complaint that his moral self-control amounts to 'slavery, not sovereignty' (*servitus . . ., non imperium*). In both texts, the figure of Seneca also characterizes Nero as an *arbiter* (*Oct.* 488; *Clem.* 1.1.2) wielding the power of life or death over his citizen subjects.

Crucially, *Octavia* follows Seneca's *On Clemency* in using Augustus as a key example, and in distinguishing between his cruel conduct as triumvir and merciful rule as *princeps*. Seneca in *Octavia* imitates his historical self in praising Augustus' capacity for political forgiveness as the basis of a long, successful reign (*Oct.* 472–81; *Clem.* 1.9–10). Nero, however, highlights Octavian's involvement in civil slaughter (504–29), which ends only with the perpetrator's exhaustion (*fessus* at *Oct.* 525 may recall Augustus' *lassa crudelitas*, 'exhausted cruelty', at *Clem.* 1.11.2). In effect, Nero repurposes material from *On Clemency* to his own ends. As Gareth Williams remarks, this amounts to a 'direct critique' of Seneca's *On Clemency*, as *Octavia*'s Nero 'turns on his former tutor by siding with the young Octavian, not the mature Augustus'.[35]

In fact, the main effect of Senecan intertexts in *Octavia* is to expose Seneca's weakness and failure as Nero's advisor. Like Atreus' minister or Thyestes, Seneca is helpless to prevent his sovereign's headstrong conduct, while the advice of his own *On Clemency* is shown to crumble against Nero's aggressive pragmatism. The image is one of a pupil who has learned to overturn his teacher's precepts, and of a teacher who has anxiously, continually predicted the scenario in which he is now placed. Yet there is also a note of optimism here because *Octavia*'s historical perspective allows us to anticipate Nero's eventual defeat. Hindsight tells us that Nero's autocratic attitudes will be his undoing, and that Seneca's counsel, however insufficient it may have seemed at the time, is fundamentally correct. History, in this case, is on the side of virtue.

Sly historical optimism also colours Nero's final appearance in the play, where he once again embodies Seneca's Atreus. Furious at the outbreak of rebellion, Nero enters the stage in full Atrean mode, chiding himself for being too slow and lenient in his response (820–6).[36] He declares death 'too light a punishment' for the populace's insubordination (*morte puniri parum est*, 825), a cry that reiterates Atreus' desire to exact punishments worse than death (*Thy.* 245–8) alongside his dismissal of traditional retribution as 'too little' (*parum est*, *Thy.* 257).[37] The foil for Nero in this scene is the praetorian prefect, who cautions against unleashing indiscriminate violence on the Roman people. But Nero boasts in reply that 'no age will forget' (*aetas nulla . . . famae eximat*, 857) the retribution he is about to pursue, a line that refers not just to his crushing the rebellion, but also, more distantly, to his supposed instigation of the great fire of 64 CE.[38] The remark echoes Atreus' self-exhortation to 'do what no future age would approve, but none would keep quiet about' (*fac quod nulla posteritas probet, / sed nulla taceat*, *Thy.* 192–3). In Atreus' case, such notoriety is achieved through the text itself, which preserves his infamous deeds for the entertainment of future audiences. Nero's reputation, however, depends not just upon the *Octavia*, but upon a broader historical record that will judge him negatively. In other words, historical context imbues his claim with unintentional irony: Nero *will* be remembered, but not in the glorious, triumphant mode he covets. History circumscribes Nero's autocratic ambitions and exposes their hollowness; the commemoration he so fiercely desires will function not as celebration, but as moral warning. *Octavia*'s awareness of this future allows us to read line 857 with a smile, knowing that Nero's iniquity will only reinforce the need for sensible, stable government. The tyrant doesn't win.

Such historical specificity is, I have shown, a major outcome of *Octavia*'s intertexts: the play envisages tight, symbiotic relationships between fictional works and the historical realities that led to their production. It uses Vergil and Lucan to explore the legacy of Augustan politics. It uses Seneca's philosophical and dramatic writings to define the moral failure of Nero's reign. Yet it also employs them to lend a patina of universality to the events depicted on stage. Allusions to Greek and Roman tragedy, and Roman epic, connect *Octavia*'s historical content to the enduring world of myth, enabling the play to claim broader applicability than mere critique of Nero's divorce. In this regard, historical and mythic material co-operate in making Nero a paradigmatic warning about the dangers of unfettered autocracy. They frame him both as a historical individual bound to a specific era, and as a cautionary model of tyranny that exceeds historical context.

3.2 History repeating

Beyond its appropriation of *Thyestes*, *Octavia*'s debt to Senecan tragedy is most apparent in its fixation upon inherited criminality and iterative suffering. The idea that wickedness recurs across generations with deterministic force, structuring characters' responses to the present, is a notable trope of Senecan drama that Anthony Boyle labels *semper idem* ('always the same').[39] It is a motif *Octavia* adapts to the Julio-Claudian household, where cyclical violence conditions how characters view themselves, their actions and their fate. There is, however, a significant element of innovation in *Octavia*'s borrowing, because the playwright uses this motif to explore not only historical determinism, but also the possibility of breaking free from past models – a prospect Senecan tragedy never entertains. *Octavia* also takes innovation a step further in using concepts of repetition at a structural level, to formulate individual scenes as reflections of each other and merge historical with dramatic iteration.

3.2.1 Cycles

History is cyclical in *Octavia*. The play depicts a world in which the hostilities enacted by former generations are repeated in the present, with scant hope of future amelioration. Octavia in particular views her circumstances as conditioned by the sequences of murder and execution that spiral down the Julio-Claudian family tree. She spends most of the opening scene situating her misery against this backdrop, as a means of emphasizing its severity and defining its origins: Messalina is condemned to death by Claudius (16–20; 265–6); Claudius murdered by Agrippina (31–2); Agrippina by Nero (126–9; 243) – why would Octavia's fate differ? The nurse concurs with her charge's pessimistic family narrative, lamenting Claudius' death at Agrippina's hand (41–4; 164–5) and Agrippina's at Nero's (45; 165–6). Although neither woman states it outright, the sequence of killings seems motivated by reparation, either on a personal or cosmic scale, with Claudius' death representing payment for Messalina's, and Agrippina's for Claudius'. The playwright enhances this impression of cyclical revenge by associating Claudius with Agamemnon: he is an all-powerful ruler who leads a large fleet (40–2) on a successful expedition of conquest (26–7) only to be murdered by a deceitful spouse (31–2; 44) and invoked by a desperate, isolated daughter (134–5).[40] The family parallel is imprecise, but the main idea is that back-and-forth vengeance will recur infinitely unless some external force intervenes. Not for the first time, the Julio-Claudians resemble the house of Atreus, and the playwright expresses a concomitantly grim view of history in which violent retaliation seems unavoidable.

Due to its reciprocal nature, vengeance tends to resist closure.[41] Only towards the first scene's end does the nurse suggest its possible cessation, when she reminds her charge, 'some avenging god will perhaps appear and a happy day will come' (*forsitan vindex deus / existet aliquis, laetus et veniet dies*, 255–6). Interpreted literally, the nurse simply hopes that divine power will intercede to save Octavia from her family's cycles of violence, but the phrase *vindex deus* may also be a submerged reference to Gaius Julius Vindex, who led an abortive rebellion against Nero in 68 CE.[42] Though unsuccessful, Vindex's rebellion signalled the demise of

Julio-Claudian domination, and his apt *cognomen* – 'Defender/ Champion/Avenger' – only heightened his association with retributive justice, whether engineered by deities or by History with a capital 'h'. Read in this way, the nurse's remark reaches beyond its immediate context to remind audiences of Nero's eventual downfall: an avenging god may not arrive for Octavia specifically, but Nero *will* be eradicated along with his family's cycles of retaliatory bloodshed. The result is a flicker of optimism in *Octavia*'s otherwise unrelenting darkness, an acknowledgement that intrafamilial revenge will cease when faced by larger, impersonal forms of redress. History won't always repeat; there is the intimation of a break with the past and a positive future beyond the Julio-Claudians.

This contrast between a positive future and grim present recurs across the play, typically in the contexts of intergenerational retribution. Agrippina's ghost is a perfect example. A hinge point between past and present, she connects two sequences of revenge and looks forward to their ultimate cessation in a future beyond the play's temporal scope. Specifically, she seeks vengeance against Nero for her own grisly murder (596; 600; 619–20) and suffers Claudius' anger over his own death and the death of Britannicus (614–17). Nero's demise is the predicted end to this sequence, functioning simultaneously as retribution *and* resolution, a way out of the otherwise endless back-and-forth of family killings. First, Agrippina imagines Claudius demanding Nero's death as recompense for Britannicus' poisoning (617). Then she depicts it on a grander scale, as cosmic/historical retribution for Nero's tyranny: 'the day and time will come when he renders up his guilty soul in payment for his crimes' (*veniet dies tempusque quo reddat suis / animam nocentem sceleribus*, 629–30). Echoing the nurse's *veniet dies* (256), Agrippina likewise anticipates a clinching moment of redress that will stop forever the repetitious cycles of Julio-Claudian aggression. The bloodied recompense of Nero's death will, paradoxically, allow history to move on.

Historical detail enhances the promise of Agrippina's vision, for besides acknowledging the general fact of Nero's death, she references specific events that correspond to the extant historical record of Nero's last days and would doubtless have been recognized by the play's contemporary audiences. Her prophecy of Nero's being forced to flee disgracefully (620), suffering tortures worse than Tantalus' thirst (621) and dying 'abandoned . . . and destitute' (*desertus . . . et cunctis egens*, 631) matches the information found in Suetonius, where the exceptional circumstances of Nero's downfall include the emperor's hasty, covert, empty-handed departure from Rome (*Nero* 48); thirstiness (*Nero* 48.3–4); and desertion by all but a few loyal slaves and freedmen (*Nero* 47.3).[43] Such specificity heightens audience consciousness of the era proceeding the play's events, and guarantees the eventual 'happy ending' that *Octavia*'s characters will not live to see: the freedom attendant on Nero's death. Once again, the drama's external frame of historical hindsight provides a gently positive counterpoint to the iterative, seemingly inescapable patterns of violence in which its characters are enmeshed.

Naturally, there is more to Roman history than the Julio-Claudians, as the play's first chorus demonstrates when it mines Rome's quasi-legendary past for examples that reflect on the Neronian present. Ideas of historical repetition feature just as prominently here as they do elsewhere in the play, but rather than enforcing suffering, they take the more hopeful form of motivating exemplary behaviour. Three allusive vignettes of Verginia (295–9), Lucretia (300–2) and Tullia (304–8) constitute the chorus' self-exhortation to match antique standards of Roman *virtus* and ensure that wrongdoing receives justice. Verginia's story comes first:[44] she is a young freeborn maiden for whom the *decemvir* Appius Claudius conceives an irrepressible lust, in pursuit of which he abuses his judicial power by trying to make her a slave – meaning he could assault her with impunity. To prevent this disgrace, Verginia's father stabs her to death. The Romans then abolish the *decemvirate* and bring Appius Claudius to trial, though he commits suicide before a verdict is reached.[45] The tale mirrors key if broad elements of Octavia's situation: a young woman is oppressed by a man's abuse of power and her suffering motivates political change.[46] Appius Claudius' potent combination of wilfulness, dominance and desire can also be seen in Nero's heedless push to marry Poppaea. But in Verginia's case, crime is punished and her ghost duly avenged (*ultique tuos sunt bene manes*, 295), which opens the possibility of vindication for Octavia as well. The chorus certainly sees it this way, using Verginia's story as encouragement to intervene in Nero's plans and alter the course of history. Hence, any suggestion of negative historical repetition is counterbalanced by the prospect of escape and improvement. The chorus treats the story as a positive model of civic activism for later generations, itself included, to imitate. It is the epitome of learning from history to avoid repeating its mistakes.

The same purpose drives the two subsequent vignettes. After Verginia, the chorus turns to Lucretia, noting her rape by Tarquin, her suicide and the civil conflict that followed. Again, the tale reflects aspects of the Nero–Octavia conflict: a tyrannous ruler's treatment of a young, innocent woman leads to popular rebellion and the ruler's eventual overthrow. Like Octavia, Lucretia is 'pitiable' (*miseranda*, 301 cf. 78; 138; 661; 907; 910; 960), while Tarquin, like Nero, is a 'savage tyrant' (*saevi . . . tyranni*, 303 cf. 87; 609–10). As a catalyst for the end of Roman monarchy and the beginning of a republican government, the event symbolizes the possibility of radical political change in response to oppression; rulers who mistreat their subjects *will* face retaliation. The chorus acknowledges as much in its praise of those forefathers who 'expelled proud kings from this city' (*reges hac expulerant / urbe superbos*, 294). Beneath the generic plural – *superbos* – is an obvious allusion to Rome's last monarch, Tarquin the Proud (*Tarquinius Superbus*), whose epithet became a byword for tyranny, and whose aggression against Lucretia the Romans duly avenged. Unspoken but ever-present in this reminiscence is the accompanying suggestion of the current populace's potential for revolutionary uprising. It has been done once, ergo it can be done again, and Nero should take heed. Lucretia's story offers a positive model for an autocrat's removal and the establishment of a more pluralistic and supposedly just governmental structure. It celebrates the power of the many against the few and accords prominence to female misery in the context of male-dominated politics, both of which elements have direct bearing on *Octavia*'s events. Historical repetition consequently acquires an optimistic as well as pessimistic form: on the one hand, tyrants continue to visit suffering on their subjects; on the other, their past defeat provides the blueprint for the chorus' revolt against Nero.

The warning culminates in the example of Tullia, Tarquin's wife, who is said to have dethroned and murdered her father before driving her chariot across the dead man's face. Connections with Nero's story are readily apparent: Tullia resembles Agrippina in her murderous pursuit of power on behalf of a close male relative, while her status as parricide recalls Nero himself. The events' broad recurrence suggests not only their inevitability, as part of an inescapable historical sequence, but their role as ciphers for the present; these are the standards by which Nero must be interpreted and judged. Significantly, their repetition also furnishes the hopeful prospect of justice. Since Tullia 'paid the penalty for her wicked crime' (*dedit infandi sceleris poenas*, 304), Nero, it is assumed, will do the same; the iterative force of revenge will, paradoxically, halt the recurrence of aristocratic criminality. From the perspective of the play's audience, of course, this is already a foregone conclusion.

Admittedly, any hint of a happy future remains slight, as the chorus dwells more on the loss of courageous civic intervention than on its recovery. The distance from republican regicide to Neronian present is measured chiefly in terms of degeneration and forgetfulness (288–92), as though earlier efforts at liberty could no longer be matched. Freedom from autocracy is counterbalanced by the 'grim war' (*bellum triste*, 300) that followed Lucretia's death, a reference that may evoke the cyclical civil conflicts so prevalent in early imperial Latin literature (not to mention Roman history!) and that would have acquired acute contemporary resonance in the wake of 69 CE. If *Octavia* really is a Flavian text, this line may be interpreted pessimistically, as acknowledgement of the internecine strife inevitably accompanying key moments of political transition in Rome. Hence, the cheerful prospect of Nero's overthrow becomes tinted by the equally conditioned prospect of civil unrest. And even in the event of success, there is no guarantee of continued political freedom. If anything, the first chorus' vignettes imply the recurring nature of Roman autocracy alongside the recurring fight to overcome it. The vision is far from rosy.

Still, such pessimism can never quite obscure the comforting possibility of change, as shown by the chorus' later decision to rebel against Nero (669–89; 780–803). Though unsuccessful, the revolt implies belief in a better future. What matters is not whether the chorus manages to reinstate Octavia, but that it tries to redirect Nero's course of action rather than remain helpless in the face of a relentlessly cyclical past. Further, as a prototype for the successful coup against Nero in 68 CE, the chorus' rebellion is itself inscribed in a positive pattern of historical iteration, providing reassurance of better luck next time.

3.2.2 Symmetries

Repetition in *Octavia* also contributes to themes of replacement and surrogacy, in reflection of the play's central event, where Nero substitutes one wife for another. This focal instance of replacement is refracted across the drama in multiple, subsidiary episodes that reduce historical cycles to specific pairings. Thus, Nero and Octavia's 'incestuous' marriage (46–7) is a doublet for Claudius and Agrippina's (141–2); Octavia assumes that the vessel conveying her to her death (906–10) is the same one used to kill Agrippina (309–55); the people tear down Poppaea's statues (683–6; 795–9) just as Nero destroyed Agrippina's following her murder (609–12); Octavia's nurse predicts that Nero will lose interest in Poppaea just as he has already lost interest in his previous mistress, Acte (193–200).[47] Besides evoking past recurrence, these symmetries overlay one character with another, alerting audiences to correspondences between figures that might otherwise appear antithetical. Poppaea might not seem to have much in common with Agrippina, but the toppling of her monuments indicates the shared problem of commemoration attendant upon (potential) displacement from power. In fact, Agrippina becomes Nero's archetypal victim in the play, her fate reverberating in the stories of Poppaea, Octavia and, in her parental/advisory role, even the story of Seneca. This means that she earns a degree of compassion from the audience even as characters within the drama criticize her; *we* feel sorry for Agrippina because, from our outside perspective, we can see how the present tragedy mirrors its immediate past. Hence, a significant effect of the play's symmetrical pairings is to generate characterological complexity through juxtaposition: aligning Octavia with Poppaea, or with Agrippina, forces audiences to consider the figures' latent similarities – similarities the characters themselves rarely if ever acknowledge.

Accompanying the idea of replacement is that of *replaceability*. By presenting individuals as versions of one another, *Octavia* explores the relationship between copies and originals and interrogates the extent to which substitutes can stand in for their prototypes. As Octavia's replacement, for instance, Poppaea is superlative in Nero's eyes (544–6; 551–2) while the chorus, by contrast, views her as a usurper who unfairly occupies Octavia's rightful position (671–3). Similar concern for authenticity colours Octavia's own experience of losing Britannicus, the brother she regards as genuine (115) and irreplaceable (178) in contrast to Nero's interloper status (*insitivus*, 249). Although Octavia herself never calls Nero 'brother', the play's insistent evocation of Jupiter and Juno as an analogy for the imperial couple (*Oct.* 219–20; 282–4; 535), alongside Octavia's reference to sisterhood (658), reminds audiences that Nero is indeed Octavia's other male sibling. This Britannicus–Nero pairing is yet another of the play's dissonant symmetries, one that measures the biological, much-loved brother against his adopted, despised counterpart and finds the copy falling far short of the original.

This theme of replication, besides enriching the play's symbolism, may reflect actual historical circumstances. For after Poppaea's death, Nero is reported first to have sought out a woman who resembled his deceased spouse, and then to have castrated and married a young slave boy, Sporus, as Poppaea's replacement (Dio 62.28.2–3). Cassius Dio remarks that Sporus, too, resembled Poppaea (62.28.2), and David Woods raises the intriguing possibility that the young man was actually named Spurius, supposedly in recognition of illegitimate parentage.[48] While Woods's hypothesis is debatable,[49] it is clear from surviving evidence that Sporus' chief role was one of substitution. Like many of *Octavia*'s characters, he stands in for someone else: a version of Poppaea, a version of a 'woman' and, possibly, a supposititious child. For whatever reason, substitution is a recurrent theme in accounts of Nero's life: he is also reported to have kept a concubine who resembled his mother, Agrippina (Suetonius *Nero* 28.2) and his death famously gave rise to impostors (Tacitus *Histories* 2.8–9; Suetonius *Nero* 57.2; Dio 66.19.3). *Octavia*'s fascination for doublings, repetition and substitution may well belong to this historical matrix of Neronian replacement.

Replication at the level of the individual is, moreover, enhanced by the play's dramaturgical symmetry, in which the entire second half of the action reflects the first. Critics have often remarked on *Octavia*'s unique 'pedimental' structure that peaks at the central appearance of Agrippina's ghost (593–645).[50] Either side of this pivotal monologue lies a corresponding sequence of scenes: Octavia's exchange with her nurse (34–272) matches Poppaea's exchange with hers (690–761); Seneca's attempt to reason with Nero (377–592) resembles the prefect's attempt to do the same (820–76); the play opens and closes with Octavia in lyric lament. Though sometimes dismissed as an overly rigid experiment in form,[51] such symmetrical arrangement is actually a clever expression of the play's content, specifically its fascination with historical recurrence. As Joseph Smith comments, *Octavia*'s structure resolves time 'into the dyad of Before and After', which 'imposes upon the audience the need to evaluate . . . comparatively'.[52] To what extent are the events following Nero's wedding an echo of those that preceded it? Similarity of the play's first and second halves implies a degree of interchangeability and overlap between Nero's victims, foreshadows future events through its acknowledgement of the past and brings us back, once again, to questions of historical inevitability. Will things ever really change?

The effects of symmetrical arrangement are most apparent in the Octavia–nurse and Poppaea–nurse scenes. Both aristocratic women claim the status of Nero's wife – former and new; both experience terrifying dreams involving their spouse; both describe their mutual mother-in-law, Agrippina, in equivalent terms; and each is accompanied by a nurse who tries to calm her charge's anxiety. In her opening lament, Octavia likens Agrippina to a Fury lighting her wedding with a Stygian torch (23–4) and Poppaea continues the idea when she recounts Agrippina's hellish appearance, shaking a bloodied torch, at the beginning of the dream that occurs on her wedding night (721–3). This repetitious imagery forges a connection between Nero's former and current wife and uses Octavia's misfortune to hint at Poppaea's: both marriages are doomed, and both will end in the woman's death. The play's dramatic 'past', i.e. the content of its earlier scenes, is used to frame and interpret its subsequent ones. By making Poppaea Octavia's dramaturgical equivalent, the playwright activates the force of historical hindsight and invites audiences to see Nero's second wife on the model of his first.

The content of the two women's dreams is also remarkably similar.[53] Octavia recounts how Britannicus' shade often appears before her in sleep, sometimes attacking Nero, sometimes fleeing in terror to Octavia's chamber (115–20). As Octavia embraces her frightened brother, Nero bursts into the room and stabs them both (121–2). Poppaea's dream, though more complex, involves similar events: it occurs in her bedchamber, albeit relocated to the underworld (726–8); it includes reunion with two deceased family members, her former husband and son (728–31); and it ends with Nero's furious violent entrance, in which he stabs either himself or Crispinus (732–3; the Latin is ambiguous). The parallel is not perfect because – as will be discussed in the proceeding section – Poppaea's dream is prophetic while Octavia's is a recurring nightmare with little foundation in actual, historical events. But the dreams' broadly similar structure links the two women's experiences, uniting them in their fear of Nero and using Octavia's circumstances to predict Poppaea's. Such resemblance to Octavia undercuts Poppaea's bid for happiness, proving that the apprehension of her dream is well founded.

Reinforcing the women's similarity is the play's innovative use of two choruses, the first loyal to Octavia, the second to Poppaea. The first chorus is involved in the on-stage action until 689 when it departs to foment a riot against Nero's new marriage. The second chorus receives less airtime: at 762–79, it performs an ode retrospectively celebrating Nero and Poppaea's wedding, and at 780–819 it receives news from the messenger of the first chorus' rampage through Rome. The first chorus then reappears at 877 singing of fame's fickleness and praising a life of humble obscurity; it remains on stage to console Octavia as she heads into exile (899–982). Although the two groups differ in their composition – the first a crowd of citizens located outside the palace; the second an assembly of courtiers stationed within[54] – they mirror each other in their respective support for Octavia and Poppaea, thereby accentuating the two women's parallel portrayal and hinting at the equivalence of their own partisanship, because the second chorus, we are given to understand, would be just as upset by Poppaea's harsh treatment as the first is by Octavia's. Such similarity is admittedly faint and relies on the audience's hindsight, but that is the game *Octavia*'s author likes to play: doubling scenes and characters in a way that prompts audiences to see historical patterns embedded in dramaturgical ones.

The last notable pair of mirror scenes are those involving Nero. Though of disproportionate lengths (the first occupies 216 lines, the second only 56), the scenes are clearly meant to be symmetrical: the first commences with an opening monologue from Seneca (377–436), followed by a combative exchange between Seneca and Nero on the topic of good government (440–592); a monologue from Nero opens the second (820–45) and the ensuing confrontation between Nero and his praetorian prefect (846–76) centres on whether the emperor should temper his harsh response to the rebellion. Both attempts at advice fail in the face of Nero's impetuous self-confidence. Parallelism is also signalled by lexical correspondence: when Nero first appears on stage at 437, he orders his prefect to 'carry out the orders' of Plautus and Sulla's executions (*perage imperata*), while his penultimate sentence at 874 demands that the prefect 'carry out orders' in subduing the rebellion (*imperata perage*).[55] The mirrored effect of the Latin confirms the scenes' reflection of each other and their need for comparative treatment.

If, following the example of Octavia and Poppaea, we read the latter of these two scenes on the model of the former, we may justifiably wonder whether the future will ever escape past patterns. Nero emerges victorious from both dialogues and stubbornly pursues his will. But, like the play's portrayal of the Roman populace, the second confrontation hints at better days to come, because the prefect who unquestioningly obeys Nero's orders at 439 finds by the second scene the courage to push back against his master. Although short-lived, his resistance indicates the fragility of Nero's power. For the audience, endowed with hindsight, it may further signal Nero's dependence upon the goodwill of the praetorian guards, who will eventually abandon the emperor and side with Galba. It is only a slight crack in the scene's 'mirror', but its consequences are huge.

3.3 Ghosts, dreams, prophecy

Octavia is a haunted play. With one ghost and two dream sequences, its events are permeated by the supernatural, creating a world of unsettled temporality and dark foreshadowing. This is a drama in which the living dream about their own deaths (Octavia at 121–2; Poppaea at 725–6) and the future is framed primarily in terms of discontinuation, i.e. of individuals and bloodlines meeting their end. Historical content complicates this perspective by merging characters' future with the audience's past and acknowledging the figures on stage as ghostly representations of their former selves. This may be a special effect of the *fabula praetexta* genre, in which re-animation of historical individuals meant unavoidable engagement with death and apparitions; *Octavia*'s handling of the past imbues it with a spectral quality independent of any thematic emphasis on the afterlife. That it employs such emphasis in addition only heightens its relationship to the realm of the dead.

3.3.1 Visions and visitations

The scene featuring Agrippina's ghost is one of the most powerful in *Octavia*. No sooner has Nero departed the stage, having decided to marry Poppaea the following day, than night falls and Agrippina materializes in the guise of a vengeful Fury. She holds a Stygian torch to light the imminent ceremony (594–7), thereby casting herself as a bridal attendant (*pronuba*) and reifying a role Octavia has already ascribed to her (23–4). In bitter terms, she excoriates Nero for murdering her and destroying her memorial statues (598–613). Her focus then shifts to Claudius: he hounds her in the underworld and demands Nero's ruin in payment for Britannicus (614–17); Agrippina promises the request's fulfilment. There follows a substantial, allusive prophecy of Nero's downfall (618–31) that seems to correlate with extant historical accounts and has been used to establish a *terminus post quem* for the play's dating.[56] Finally, Agrippina becomes despondent, admitting she feels helpless before the sheer monstrosity of her son's deeds and wishing she had died before giving birth (632–43). The speech's final contrafactual image has Agrippina descend to the underworld together with the unborn Nero, who, innocent and still joined to his mother, gazes on his famous forebears – men who will now revile him for blackening the family's reputation (639–43). The speech is a bravura expression of malevolence and resentment.

In her knowledgeable and vengeful stance, Agrippina's ghost has much in common with the stage spectres of Renaissance tragedy, whose chief motivation is the pursuit of extrajudicial justice – most often for themselves – and who are so fully informed about the past that they frequently perform an expositional role for the tragedies' audiences.[57] Such characteristics are primarily Senecan in origin: both *Octavia*'s Agrippina and her Renaissance counterparts owe a clear debt to Senecan tragedy,[58] which abounds in ghosts and tends to depict them as omniscient figures detached from yet overseeing events played out on stage. In comparison to Greek tragedy, which features only three on-stage spectres across a corpus of 31 extant plays,[59] Senecan drama revels in disembodiment, hellishness and haunting: *Thyestes* opens in the underworld, with the shade of Tantalus,

Agamemnon with the shade of Thyestes; Laius' ghost is described at length in *Oedipus*; Hector's and Achilles' spectral appearances are reported in *Troades*; and Absyrtus haunts his sister in *Medea*. A similarly morbid atmosphere envelops *Octavia*, where boundaries between life and death seem indistinct, and the horrors of the underworld shift from metaphor to reality. *Octavia*'s Agrippina resembles her Senecan counterparts in reviling herself (*Oct.* 645; cf. *Ag.* 22–36) as well as her offspring (*Oct.* 598–643; cf. *Thy.* 18–23; *Oed.* 634–58); in stressing her murky underworld provenance (*Oct.* 593–5 and 644; cf. *Ag.* 1–4 and 12–21; *Thy.* 1–23); and in her general fascination for crime and the grotesque. She also follows them in possessing and communicating knowledge of events beyond the present moment: both Thyestes in *Agamemnon* (37–52) and Laius in *Oedipus* (647–58) allude to the future, elliptically yet accurately, while Tantalus in *Thyestes* contents himself with a broad acknowledgement of worse crimes to come (18–20). Unsurprisingly, two of these Senecan ghosts function as prologues, while the third appears in a protracted quasi-messenger speech;[60] in other words, all three fulfil a narrative function in which the ghost's superior knowledge is a substitute for the author's. This is likewise true of Agrippina, whose historically informed vision places her above the play's other characters.

Of the Greek tragic ghosts, only Polydorus in Euripides' *Hecuba* fulfils a similarly expositional role. Darius in Aeschylus' *Persians*, by contrast, does not know and must be informed of his son's defeat, and Clytemnestra in Aeschylus' *Eumenides* is more embedded in the play's action, pursuing revenge but expressing no prophetic vision of the future. Yet Greek tragedy's influence cannot entirely be discounted from *Octavia*'s ghost episode, at least in regard to content rather than form, because the play often likens Agrippina to Clytemnestra, and this scene reinforces the parallel by focusing on a mother's desire for retaliation against a murderous son. Like Aeschylus' Clytemnestra, Agrippina's ghost is associated with the Furies and their expiation of blood guilt; she also admits to being attacked in the afterlife for her crimes (614–17), which may evoke Clytemnestra's complaint of being taunted in the underworld on account of her killings (Aeschylus' *Eumenides* 96–8). Though slender, these connections seem probable given *Octavia*'s pervasive use of Greek tragedy. Their presence is also made more likely by the surrounding context of Neronian mythmaking, which assimilated Nero to Orestes and Agrippina to Clytemnestra.[61] For instance, Suetonius numbers 'Orestes the matricide' among the emperor's favourite stage roles (*Nero* 21.3); reports a graffito that links Orestes and Nero as matricides (*Nero* 39.2); and relates that Nero himself felt hounded by his mother's ghost and a contingent of Furies (*Nero* 34.4). The myth was clearly a touchstone for Nero's actions; its distant yet persistent citation in *Octavia* belongs within this cultural framework.

From Agrippina's ghost it is a short step to Poppaea's dream, which occurs the following night, after the wedding. The scene begins with the nurse wondering at her charge's sudden distress. Poppaea replies that she has seen in her sleep a crowd of mourning Roman matrons, led by Agrippina in the role of a Fury (718–23). Poppaea follows her new husband's mother only to plunge through an abyss into the underworld, where she sees her marriage bed and sinks down on it, exhausted (724–8). Another crowd now advances towards her, including her first husband, Rufrius Crispinus, and the couple's young son (728–30). Poppaea and Crispinus embrace but at that moment Nero bursts in, armed with a sword, which he buries either in his own throat, or Crispinus' (730–3). I have noted in the immediately preceding section of this chapter the dream's similarity to Octavia's account of her own nightmare, in which Britannicus, terrified, seeks safety in his sister's chamber. As the siblings cling to each other, Nero bursts in and kills them both with a single sword thrust (120–2). The two dreams are equivalent in highlighting the dreamer's fear, depicting reunion with lost family members, and ending with Nero's furious, violent entrance.[62]

But Poppaea's is also more complex than Octavia's and arguably exhibits a prophetic quality that aligns it with Agrippina's speech.[63] The nightmare can be read as a vision of the future, as yet another example of *Octavia*'s playwright overlaying dramatic time with historical time and prompting audiences to perceive both simultaneously.

Poppaea's dream becomes prophetic if viewed as an historical sequence of deaths.[64] Poppaea is first: her sudden descent to the underworld, while surrounded by a ceremonial throng of Roman women, combines wedding with funeral imagery to suggest the fatal outcome of her union with Nero.[65] Poppaea would die in 65 CE, after Nero kicked her during pregnancy (Suet. *Nero* 35.3; Tac. *Annals* 16.6).[66] With Poppaea situated in the afterlife, the next people to arrive in the dream sequence are Crispinus senior and junior, the former forced to commit suicide in 66 CE, in the aftermath of the Pisonian conspiracy, and the latter drowned on Nero's orders.[67] The final death in this catalogue is Nero's, who on this reading enters and stabs himself: *irrupit intra tecta cum trepidus mea / ensemque iugulo condidit saevum Nero* ('when Nero, fearful, burst into my chamber and plunged a savage sword in his throat' 732–3). Lack of a personal pronoun in the Latin makes it unclear whether Nero attacks Crispinus or himself (*suo* or *eius*?),[68] but the latter option is strengthened by chronology, i.e. by Nero's death following all the others, and by correspondence with the historical record, which reports Nero as having died by a self-inflicted stab wound to the throat (Suet. *Nero* 49.3). Nonetheless, valid caveats remain, because Poppaea's dream is otherwise vague about people's *modes* of death – in keeping with the medium's symbolic qualities – and because Nero performs an equivalent, unhistorical stabbing at the conclusion to Octavia's dream (122). In fact, treating the passage as deliberately ambiguous may be the most profitable approach, since this allows us to appreciate both its prediction of Nero's ruin and its evocation of his violent, jealous nature.[69] As a glimpse of the future, it is also coloured by Poppaea's present anxiety.

A major effect of this prophetic material is to complicate the play's temporality by introducing a level of historical time beyond the characters' knowledge. To some extent, of course, this is a permanent feature of all historical fiction, which acknowledges and incorporates audience hindsight as a sometimes ironic, sometimes sympathetic counterpoint to its immediate narrative. In Poppaea's case, the historical long view of her dream adds pathos to her present circumstances and makes her pitiable, as the suggestion of Nero's murderous rampages and gruesome end subvert newlywed happiness. When the nurse subsequently attempts to interpret Poppaea's dream (740–53), hindsight acquires an ironic quality, undermining her optimistic predictions of Neronian peace (752–3) and making her seem foolish. The effect is different again for Agrippina, because as a ghost she already exists beyond the frame of mortal time.[70] Her appearance on stage represents the past's temporary eruption into the present, while her prophecy invites audiences to contemplate 'history in the future tense'.[71] The audience views *backwards* what the characters in the tragedy live *forwards*. The result is an enhanced sense of audience and authorial omniscience, as our superior perspective is constantly, indirectly invoked in contrast to the figures on stage who cannot see what lies ahead and seem more restrictively time-bound in the sense that their stories have already been completed.

3.3.2 Ghosts on stage

Octavia's ghostliness is not confined only to spectral appearances on stage and in dreams; it permeates the entire play and floats behind every character like a sinister shadow. The basic reason for this, once again, is the drama's historical content: all the named individuals portrayed in *Octavia* were dead by 68 CE, so their representation on stage, even for the work's earliest, Galban dating, was a form of resurrection. Octavia, Nero, Seneca and Poppaea resemble ghosts in being re-embodied and brought forward to address an audience.[72] The play's emphasis on needing to remember these individuals – Nero as a negative example; Poppaea, Octavia and Seneca as his victims – likewise contributes to their ghostly quality of insubstantial permanence and chimes with the ghost's typical desire to imprint its presence on the mind of the living.

Octavia is the most overtly spectral figure in the drama. She refers to herself as an *umbra* ('shade/shadow', 71) and repeatedly anticipates joining other shades in death (79; 958). As an individual, she seems to occupy the margins of her own life, grieving for the past and framing the future only in terms of her ruin (101; 174; 653) or Nero's (174). Further enhancing this portrayal is her inability or unwillingness to have children with Nero, which delimits her continued existence and accentuates the threat of mortality. When the nurse urges Octavia to reconcile with Nero, 'so that you may restore your father's falling house with children' (*labentem ut domum / genitoris olim subole restituas tua*, 179–80), Octavia replies that that future is already, irrevocably closed: Poppaea will give Nero a child, while Octavia feels drawn to join her deceased brother (181–2). Seneca's similarly hopeful forecast of Octavia filling the palace with Nero's offspring (533–4) works as a counterfactual future, enticing yet impossible, that throws Octavia's morbid perspective into even sharper relief. In this drama, where hope of imperial children represents the ultimately unrealized continuance of the Julio-Claudian dynasty, Octavia and Nero's childlessness is a symbol not only of their doomed marriage, but of their own erasure.

Octavia's ghostliness is also conveyed through the drama's motifs of light and dark. As Giancarlo Mazzoli has noted, the heroine's preference for night over day connects her to the world of the dead.[73] Her opening speech declares the daylight 'eternally hostile' (*semper funesta*, 18) and 'more loathed than the darkness' (*tenebris invisa magis*, 20),[74] while her presence at dawn, as the play's first speaker, renders her analogous to a ghost. The trope of ghosts appearing in the very early morning and heralding the tragedy's action is well established in Seneca: both Tantalus and Thyestes feature in the opening scenes of their respective dramas, at a time immediately before daybreak (*Thy.* 120–1; *Ag.* 53–6). Polydorus, too, performs the same function in Euripides' *Hecuba* (1–58), appearing at daybreak to provide the tragedy's backstory and anticipate its events. Agrippina in *Octavia* likewise materializes on the morning of Nero and Poppaea's wedding, presumably prior to sunrise,[75] and signals the beginning of the second day's action. Notably, *Octavia*'s author employs a dawn scene for each of the three days that comprise the drama's plot, with Poppaea's dream initiating the events of the third and final day. This parallel – Octavia, Agrippina, Poppaea – situates the play's heroine in the shadowy context of night-time, dreams and haunting, a region she expresses no desire to escape.

Broader evocation of ghosts is likely to have emerged in performance, through *Octavia*'s use of masks. I argued above in Chapter 1 section 3 ('History on stage') that performances of *fabulae praetextae* must have called for specific masks modelled on individual faces, and in the case of Neronian Rome, we are lucky enough to have independent evidence that comes close to corroborating this hypothesis: Suetonius (*Nero* 21.3) and Cassius Dio (63.9.5) report that Nero sometimes performed on stage in a mask representing his own face or that of the deceased Poppaea. These anecdotes indicate that a) portrait-masks existed; b) they could be worn on stage, though the reports clearly portray Nero's behaviour as exceptional; and c) they may have been linked to or evoked Roman aristocratic funeral practices. Nero's donning the image of his dead wife is strikingly similar to the Roman custom of professional actors wearing *imagines* (wax death masks) and impersonating deceased ancestors in the funeral procession. Accounts in Polybius (*Histories* 6.53.5–7), Diodorus (31.25.2) and Suetonius (*Vespasian* 19.2) testify to the fidelity of such performances, which reproduced the peculiarities of the individual's gait and appearance and, in the case of Vespasian's impersonator, the emperor's renowned stinginess (*Vespasian* 19.2).[76] It seems probable that *praetexta* drama recalled these funeral customs through its required impersonation of actual, historical figures and its complementary emphasis on aristocratic lineage. Although *imagines* themselves may not have resembled theatrical masks and did not have a primarily dramatic purpose – they were meant to be displayed in the *atria* of wealthy households, as a visual family tree[77] – association could easily have gone the other way, with *Octavia* seeming funereal through the simple fact of its actors re-embodying the dead and wearing masks of their faces. Having someone appear on stage in the guise of the recently deceased Nero is undeniably spooky, and that spookiness increases when situated against a cultural backdrop of death masks and professional impersonation of the dead. Like actors wearing *imagines* as part of the Roman burial process, *Octavia*'s performers must have engaged in an exercise of quasi-resurrection, re-animating the dead in ghostly outline and affording them a presence both immediate and insubstantial. Nero, Octavia, Seneca and Poppaea are ghosts on stage, even in the absence of the drama's haunted, subterranean imagery.[78]

This phantasmal aspect of *Octavia*'s staging may find correlation in the play's frequent references to characters' faces.[79] When Octavia complains that 'looking upon the tyrant's swollen and savage face is a punishment worse than death' (*poena nam gravior nece est / videre tumidos et truces . . . / vultus tyranni*, 108–10), her commonplace expression of fear can also function meta-dramatically, as acknowledgement of Nero's likeness being presented on stage and of the audience having to confront this image. Considered in terms of performance, a face-to-face encounter with Nero involves issues of commemoration, representation and posthumous reanimation – all potentially unsettling or contentious prospects for an audience with recent, living memories of the emperor. A similar nexus of commemoration, masking conventions and ghostliness may be present in the second choral ode, where the enraged populace vents its hatred of Poppaea:

Gravis en oculis undique nostris
iam Poppaeae fulget imago
   iuncta Neroni.
affligat humo violenta manus
similes nimium vultus dominae
ipsamque toris detrahat altis,

Look, oppressing our eyes everywhere
Poppaea's image gleams,
   Paired with Nero's.
Let our violent hands dash to the ground
That visage all too similar to our mistress's
And drag the woman herself from her high couch

Octavia 682–7

In distinguishing Poppaea from her image, the chorus recognizes a gap between representation and reality: the *imago* and *vultus* are not Poppaea per se, but extremely faithful likenesses acting as substitutes for her living, breathing self. Their simultaneous resemblance to and reflection of Poppaea assimilates them to the status of ghosts that at once evoke and do not fully capture their antecedent individual. These images both are and are not Poppaea, and although context suggests the chorus refers to statuary,[80] it is tempting to hear in the term *imago* (683) an echo of Roman funeral traditions, which Poppaea's on-stage embodiment could easily have recalled. The reference could in fact be anticipatory, because 'Poppaea' – i.e. an actor wearing a mask of her face – will feature in the immediately following scene, a dramaturgical move that prompts comparison between the chorus' description and the figure presented on stage. The audience, too, gazes upon not Poppaea herself but her likeness (cf. *similes nimium vultus dominae*, 686). Hence, the chorus' remarks heighten awareness of dramatic illusion and its potentially spectral atmosphere, focusing attention on Poppaea's face to underscore her insubstantial presence and possibly – distantly – evoke the Roman custom of *imagines*. Poppaea, we are reminded, is already dead.

3.4 Nero's victims

Ghosts want to be remembered; they typically haunt the living to remind them of their grievances and dues. To the extent that *Octavia* is populated by ghosts, therefore, it is also a play about memory and commemoration.[81] From its portrayal of characters reliving past trauma to its recurrent interest in monuments and statuary, *Octavia* examines how history is memorialized and by whom. At a synoptic level, it also strives to preserve the voices and stories of some of Nero's most prominent victims, allowing them to give their own version of events less for the sake of contesting the historical record than actively intervening to modify it. The play itself is an exercise in memory that draws attention to processes of commemoration at the same time as it engages in them.

3.4.1 Preventing erasure

When *Octavia*'s first chorus chides itself for forgetfulness (*nos … immemores*, 288), it signals not just its own recent failure to defend Claudius' memory, but also the drama's broader concern with how to recall the past. What one chooses to remember is a problem to which *Octavia* presents no uniform solution, encompassing as it does examples from obsessive recollection to aggressive destruction. Though the play errs on the side of preservation, it clearly portrays unceasing remembrance as an unhealthy state, a verdict that applies to Octavia above all. The heroine begins the play with the exhortation to 'resume customary grief' (*repete assuetos . . . questus*, 6): she declares the need to lament Messalina eternally (*semper genetrix deflenda mihi*, 'o mother always mourned by me', 10), moans that her mother's death has buried her 'in everlasting sorrow' (*perpetuo . . ./ luctu*, 267–8) and describes herself as 'eternally recalling [her] deceased brother'" (*semper fratris extincti memor*, 226). The nurse joins her in referring to Britannicus as an 'unfortunate boy, to be mourned forever by us' (*deflende nobis semper, infelix puer*, 167). Such promises of perpetual grief can, on the one hand, be interpreted as rebellious acts designed to preserve the memory of imperial victims against the wishes of the prevailing regime. Britannicus' commemoration certainly fits this model: as a rival successor, murdered by Nero, he becomes a symbol of resistance in the fight against tyranny. The more his innocence is emphasized (166–73) the more his memory blackens Nero's reputation. Messalina, although a more morally complex case, likewise reflects poorly on Claudius: her brutal execution, witnessed by Octavia (16–17), tears the family apart and facilitates Nero's displacement of Claudius' biological children. Hence remembering her becomes, inter alia, a way to portray Nero as an undeserving outsider whose rule is illegitimate.

But commemoration, no matter how deep and persistent, remains a passive form of resistance, and Octavia's incessant lament is thematically linked to her futility, as someone who cannot detach herself from the past. To the extent that it governs Octavia's obsession with death, memory in the play's first scene becomes an unbearable weight that must be shifted to make room for the future. Historical preservation, the drama implies from its outset, is a necessarily selective process, at its most effective when it balances the demands of the dead and the living, granting the latter space to grow.

Complementing these instances of individual reminiscence is *Octavia*'s fascination with monumental acts of public commemoration. Appropriately for an historical drama, *Octavia* situates its own memorializing venture against a backdrop of architectural, sculptural and inscriptional tributes, implicitly comparing their stony permanence with drama's multivalent, multivocal approach. A neat example is Octavia's condemnation of Agrippina as a 'wicked parent' (*infanda parens*, 92), who, despite being murdered by Nero, 'will bear this title after death, for all eternity' (*feret hunc titulum post fata . . . / . . . longo semper in aevo*, 96–7). The image at 96–7 is of a commemorative inscription summarizing Agrippina's achievements,[82] or in this case, her misdeeds. Octavia imagines Agrippina's memory being recorded as a negative example, an idea that activates parallel awareness of the play's own commemorative enterprise. How does Octavia's memory of Agrippina, which she wants to embed in the official record, compare to the drama's treatment, which likewise aspires to the status of history? Significantly, the two views diverge, for although *Octavia* makes no attempt to hide Agrippina's iniquity, it nonetheless encourages sympathy for her, alongside Octavia, Poppaea and Seneca, as another of Nero's victims. No matter how unpleasant Agrippina is as an individual, her death is memorialized as a negative comment on Nero's reign (309–76; 598–608), in direct contrast to Octavia's judgement (91–7). In this regard, the play subsumes Octavia's literally inflexible verdict within a broader matrix of historical understanding. It celebrates its own capacity to supplement and complicate the epigraphic record, and ultimately, to confer a greater level of permanence.

Octavia's role in preserving memory is also a prominent theme in the speech of Agrippina's ghost. Here, Agrippina complains of Nero attacking her monuments after her murder: 'the savage tyrant rages against his mother's name, he wants to obliterate my services, he destroys the statues and inscriptions that commemorate me throughout the whole world' (*saevit in nomen ferus / matris tyrannus, obrui meritum cupit, / simulacra, titulos destruit memores mei / totum per orbem*, 609–12).[83] The destruction she envisages resembles the Roman practice of memory sanctions (often erroneously called *damnatio memoriae*), which involved erasing the former public tributes, typically names and effigies, of disgraced individuals.[84] As has been noted, Agrippina's protest is historically odd given that the memory sanctions enacted after her death were minimal and haphazard; visual evidence of her influence would still have been readily apparent to *Octavia*'s contemporary audience in Rome.[85] But her remarks are better understood not as reflecting the material conditions consequent upon her fall, but as part of the drama's own competitive impulse towards commemoration. Evocation of memory sanctions, no matter how historically inaccurate, is a potent way of conveying Agrippina's threatened erasure from the public record. It also encapsulates Nero's tyrannical desire to control public commemoration and bend history to his will, a desire *Octavia* opposes and overrides at every level. Once again, the play positions itself against the supposed permanence of monuments and epigraphic material, preserving Agrippina's memory and allowing her to speak even in the face of Nero's attempt to obliterate her.

Anxieties about memory and commemoration likewise inform the play's portrayal of choral rebellion against Poppaea, in which the rioting Roman populace topples her statues and smashes them limb from limb (682–6; 794–9). While the violence visited upon her effigies is clearly metonymy for the hatred borne towards Poppaea's person, the citizens' attack also resembles the demolition and mutilation of statues attendant upon Roman memory sanctions. Anthony Boyle notes comparable examples of Sejanus' images being destroyed in 31 CE (Dio 58.11.3; Juvenal 10.58–113) and Domitian's in 96 (Suetonius *Domitian* 23.1; Pliny *Panegyric* 52.4–6), approximately a generation after *Octavia*.[86] This hint of memory sanctions further emerges from the passages' focus on Poppaea's face (*vultus* at 686; *ora* at 795), which besides potentially acknowledging her beauty or working as a periphrastic identification of the statue's image, may recall the targeted erasure of facial representations following an individual's fall from grace.[87] And even if we stop short of interpreting this passage in terms of memory sanctions, the chorus' attack upon Poppaea's statues still threatens to negate her public presence and, hence, her claim to a prominent place in history. The tearing down and smashing of her sculptures represents the dismantling of her political and cultural worth, as well as being an expression of popular dissent.

In contrast to the chorus' hostility, *Octavia* portrays itself as rescuing Poppaea's memory from oblivion, principally by allowing her to speak and concentrating attention on her personal experience of events, which belies the chorus' mono-dimensional viewpoint. As in its treatment of Agrippina, the drama balances the individual woman's voice against others' opinions of her, not with the facile aim of exoneration, but to ensure fuller coverage of the past. *Octavia* aspires to replace, or at very least compete with, other assessments of Nero's reign, which leads it in this case to diverge from the chorus. The difference is noteworthy because the play's perspective often seems to be aligned with the citizen chorus', and scholars tacitly assume that the discontented populace functions as a mouthpiece for the playwright.[88] In this instance, however, the play implies that the chorus acts erroneously, because even though the chorus demonstrates laudable anti-tyrannical sentiment, its aggression towards public memory conflicts with *Octavia*'s central aim of remembering Nero's victims and according them a rightful place in history.

Nor is this commemoration restricted to the play's speaking characters. As has already been noted, other Neronian victims feature in *Octavia*'s dialogues: Rubellius Plautus (437); Faustus Cornelius Sulla (438); Rufrius Crispinus (729–31) and his son (729–30); and the ever-present Britannicus (62–9; 103; 112–22; 166–73; 178; 182; 268–9). But the drama puts these men in at best auxiliary roles and displays a marked preference for safeguarding the memory of imperial women. Notably, all the play's references to inscriptions and statuary occur in the context of female commemoration; Octavia, Agrippina and Poppaea are all somehow associated with public forms of memorialization. Even Acte, a freedwoman and Nero's erstwhile mistress, is described as 'erecting memorials that testify to her fear' (*monumenta extruit / quibus timorem fassa testatur suum*, 196–7). While the passage's meaning is opaque at best – what does Acte fear and how is that apprehension connected to her commissioning of a monument?[89] – the general idea seems linked to the theme of women's memorials, which acquires prominence in *Octavia*, not just as a result of its female-centric take on Julio-Claudian history but also, most likely, in tacit acknowledgement of the Julio-Claudians having been the first to introduce public memory sanctions against women.[90] The contested commemoration of women, their preservation as behavioural examples, and their presence in epigraphy and sculpture is portrayed by *Octavia* as a defining aspect of the Julio-Claudian principate.

The final note in this grim threnody is the chorus' closing catalogue of Julio-Claudian female *exempla*: Agrippina the Elder (932–40); Claudius' sister, Livilla (941–3); her daughter, Julia (944–6); Messalina (947–51); and Nero's mother, Agrippina the Younger (952–7). I have already discussed this passage for its possible intertextual echoes of Sophocles' *Antigone*, but it has another function as well: as a succinct, chronological list that records the names and fates of Octavia's prominent female forebears, this choral catalogue resembles a eulogy and has a distinctly epitaphic tone.[91] The genitive phrases it employs to define women's marriage status – 'Caesar's wife' (*Caesaris uxor*, 934) for Agrippina the Elder; 'Drusus' Livia' (*Livia Drusi*, 941) for Livilla – are typical epigraphic language, corroborated by extant inscriptions.[92] The chorus' labelling Agrippina the Younger 'Nero's great parent' (*parens tanta Neronis*, 953) likewise seems to recall epigraphic formulae honouring Agrippina's motherhood: *Neronis Caesaris mater* ('mother of Nero Caesar') and *mater Augusti* ('mother of Augustus') were common phrases on early Neronian coinage, while inscriptions often celebrated Nero and his mother in tandem.[93]

Such language embeds this choral ode within the play's broader themes of memorialization and preservation: it highlights *Octavia*'s role in shaping and conveying cultural memories, and implicitly measures that role against the supposed permanence of public tributes. As a vehicle of collective memory, the chorus in the final scene incorporates and supersedes epigraphic material, performing an equivalent function of perpetuating stories from the past while additionally demonstrating that these memories are everyone's mutable property, not just the preserve of a select few. The chorus' treatment transforms the stories of these Julio-Claudian women from their limited, partial expression in inscriptions to dynamic reflections of Octavia's own fate that command our sympathy even in instances of moral transgression. Lapidary commemoration provides the basis for, but is ultimately surpassed by, the elasticity of communal, multivocal memories.

The other main purpose of monuments and inscriptions in *Octavia* is to symbolize the official version of history, the record created by and in the service of the emperor: Nero controls both the bestowal and removal of public memory in the play (as witnessed by Agrippina's ghost), and rebellion against him is articulated as a direct assault on officially endorsed memorials (as witnessed by the chorus and messenger). Even Octavia, when she hopes for Agrippina's enduringly negative commemoration, aspires to control how the past is regarded. The play, in contrast, sets out to rewrite and destabilize these official narratives, introducing the plurality of viewpoints in which drama excels and allowing historical perspective to shrink Nero's ambitions. Though no less biased or hopeful of its story dominating the historical landscape, *Octavia* sets out to correct the Neronian narrative by refocusing popular attention on what – it feels – really needs to be remembered.

3.4.2 Being heard

As noted in the preceding section, a large part of *Octavia*'s commemorative impulse involves giving Nero's victims a voice, allowing their experiences of the *princeps* to be heard and preserved.

Drama is the perfect medium for this because it creates the illusion of characters being able to speak for themselves, without the obvious presence of authorial control. The impression is still more pronounced in the case of historical drama – especially for plays dealing with recent events – because the incontrovertible fact of the characters' previous existence lends them an extra layer of reality and independence. Despite their obviously stylized speech and adherence to dramatic conventions, they convey a strong sense of personal presence, of embodiment or – more pertinently for *Octavia* – resurrection.

Of all the play's characters, Octavia benefits most from this historicized reimagining, for the surviving historical record accords her not a single word. Her role in Cassius Dio's *Roman History* is minimal and functional albeit with the crucial caveat that Dio's account survives only in epitomized form. Her role in Suetonius is likewise restricted, amounting to a few brief comments on Nero's divorce (*Nero* 35.1–3), a sensationalized report about Nero being haunted by Octavia's ghost (46.1) and the observation that Nero died on the anniversary of Octavia's murder (57.1). Tacitus grants her more attention, in line with his expansive narrative, but even here Octavia is prominently mute. In illustration of her youth and vulnerability, she is constantly subject to others' wishes: she is a pawn in Messalina's desperate attempt to evade execution (*Annals* 11.32–4); treated as an advantageous match for Agrippina's son (12.3, 12.9, 12.58); cowed by Nero's violence (13.16); and driven into divorce and death by Poppaea's relentless ambition (14.1, 14.60–3). She has, Tacitus reports, learned to hide her thoughts and feelings for fear of reprisal (13.16). The only time Tacitus comes close to letting Octavia speak is when he describes the pleas uttered prior to her execution, and even then her entreaty is not framed as direct speech: 'she protested that she was now husbandless, and only a sister, and she invoked the family of Germanicus, which she shared with Nero, and finally the name of Agrippina' (*cum iam viduam se et tantum sororem testaretur communisque Germanicos et postremo*

Agrippinae nomen cieret, *Annals* 14.64). Octavia's voicelessness seems all the starker when compared with Tacitus' Agrippina and Poppaea, both of whom speak frequently and forcefully, especially to Nero. That *Octavia*'s playwright chose to position this young, defenceless heroine alongside two traditionally vocal women, and to let her express her resentment, her dread and her forbearance, indicates a concerted effort to enhance her presence and consequently, her place in people's memories.

The conspicuousness accorded to women's voices in *Octavia* may also derive from the work's affiliation with tragedy, a genre in which female characters traditionally claimed prominent speaking roles.[94] *Octavia*'s grafting of tragic form onto historical subject matter is doubtless the reason for its focus not only on female speech, but specifically on female lament, as Octavia, Agrippina and Poppaea are all represented in various states of mourning and distress. In turn, this provides a partial explanation for the play's sympathetic handling of such otherwise forthright figures as Agrippina and Poppaea: tragedy demands portrayal of their suffering, which encourages a somewhat compassionate response from the audience, in contrast to the antipathy their brashness tends to provoke in Tacitus.

But even if tragedy is the primary cause of *Octavia*'s focus on women, the play's interaction with collective and historical memory remains an important factor. Its portrayal of Agrippina, for instance, besides enhancing the drama's tragic atmosphere, is also designed to ameliorate (or at least, complicate) her posthumous reputation. Once again, *Octavia* achieves this end through drama's inherent plurality of viewpoints: it begins with Octavia's hostile portrait of her stepmother (21–33; 93–7), which the first chorus then tempers in its protracted account of Agrippina's death (309–76). The direct speech granted to Agrippina in this latter narrative intensifies the impression of her victimhood and hence, her claim on the audience's pity. She complains of Nero's ingratitude (332–3) before confessing she deserves this fate as punishment for having made him emperor (334–7) and invoking Claudius to lift his head from hell to rejoice in her drowning (338–44). She speaks again in the ode's closing stanza when Nero's henchman arrives to assassinate her:

> rogat infelix,
> utero dirum condat ut ensem:
> 'hic est, hic est fodiendus' ait
> 'ferro, monstrum qui tale tulit.'
>
> Ill-fated, she asks him
> To bury his sword in her womb:
> 'this,' she says, 'strike this with your blade,
> The place that bore such a monster.'
>
> *Octavia* 369–72

Alongside their demonstrably tragic pedigree (echoing, most immediately, Seneca's Jocasta at *Oedipus* 1038–9),[95] Agrippina's words also draw attention to her individual suffering, shifting her portrayal from power-hungry virago to brave, self-aware and seemingly repentant parent. By giving her a voice, no matter how stylized, the playwright invites a different perspective on Agrippina, one that tries to understand and retain her side of the story.

This perspective is strengthened by Agrippina's subsequent appearance on stage and delivery of a speech that correlates with the chorus' account. As in the first choral ode, Agrippina describes the night of her shipwreck (598–604), apostrophizes Claudius (618) and expresses regret at her son's criminality (632–5; 642–3). Similarities between the two passages generate the illusion of authenticity, as though the chorus really had channelled Agrippina's thoughts. Further, the ghost's admission of perpetual remembrance – *manet inter umbras impiae caedis mihi / semper memoria* ('the memory of my impious murder persists for me even in death,' 598–9) – suggests the interrelationship of being heard and being commemorated. Agrippina's refusal to forget corresponds at an extra-dramatic level to the play's commemorative purpose, reminding audiences of the continued need to recall Nero's crimes and prevent death from obliterating his victims.

Alongside Agrippina and Octavia, Poppaea is also granted an individual voice in this play, one that differs substantially from the extant historical record. Unlike Tacitus, who depicts Poppaea as malicious and unscrupulous in her ambition, *Octavia*'s playwright chooses to emphasize Poppaea's victimhood: her uncertainty and trepidation. Boyle rightly notes that the parallel composition of the Octavia–nurse and Poppaea–nurse scenes could have been used to highlight the women's differences (e.g. in terms of age, confidence, sexual experience), but the playwright focuses on affinities instead.[96] *This* Poppaea emerges as a reverent individual who pays due respect to the gods (756–61), expresses genuine affection for Nero (716) and is concerned about what her dream portends not just for herself but for others (739).[97] Whereas Tacitus' Poppaea is the chief instigator of Octavia's execution (*Annals* 14.60–4) and the detail of her needing to gaze upon Octavia's severed head (14.64) likens her to an archetypal tyrant,[98] Poppaea in *Octavia* never once mentions her rival, and it is Nero, not his new wife, who demands Octavia's decapitation (861). The aggression that Poppaea displays in Tacitus appears to have been transferred to Nero in this play, especially in the scene with the praetorian prefect (844–76), while the Poppaea presented on stage expresses only fear. In this way, her voice becomes yet another index of sympathy for Nero's victims and recollection of their suffering.

Such sympathetic treatment extends even to Seneca, Nero's only male victim to claim a speaking role in this play.[99] While his portrayal is doubtless not driven by the same commemorative urgency as Octavia's – for Seneca's prominence as Nero's advisor (*amicus principis*) alongside his voluminous written output and distinctive literary 'voice' all but assured his posthumous remembrance – nonetheless the play's portrait seems to encourage an appreciative assessment of Seneca and his role in the Neronian regime, and it does so chiefly by allowing him to speak. In contrast to Dio's famous denunciation of Seneca's supposed hypocrisy (61.10.2–4) which includes his labelling Seneca a 'tyrant teacher' (τυραννοδιδάσκαλος, 61.10.2), and Tacitus' largely critical image of Seneca as a slippery statesman whose actions often belied his philosophical principles,[100] *Octavia*'s depiction is predominantly positive: *this* Seneca is firm and rational, if somewhat pessimistic, and his advice to Nero echoes the moral precepts expressed in his written works. I have already discussed (in 3.1.3 'Seneca') how *Octavia*'s Seneca quotes from his own *On Clemency*, which the playwright uses both to illustrate the historical Seneca's ultimate failure to control his pupil and to validate the philosopher's moral stance. To these outcomes we may add the further effect of uniting Seneca's deeds with his words, for by having the figure of Seneca quote his own work, the playwright depicts a man who practices what he preaches. Besides simply enhancing the 'Senecan' quality of his characterization, these allusions join Seneca the statesman seamlessly to Seneca the philosopher, in contravention of his more well-known historical portrait as an insincere opportunist. While it is impossible to gauge from the scant remains of contemporary historiography whether *Octavia*'s version of Seneca aims at contesting or influencing concurrent historical accounts, the portrait certainly belongs within the play's broader commemorative celebration of Nero's victims. By presenting Seneca 'in person' (so to speak) and having him articulate the case for self-restraint before a heedless, hot-headed *princeps*, *Octavia* reminds its audiences of Seneca's potential value as an advisor, and of the great loss his death represented for the regime. The scene preserves Nero's iniquity, too, while its citation of Seneca's precepts pays regretful homage to the ideal of a peaceful, stable reign that Nero failed to fulfil.

Besides these individual victims, the play memorializes the collective suffering of the Roman people in the form of a chorus that voices its opposition to the prevailing regime, acts on this impulse, endures violent retaliation and returns in a final show of support for the play's beleaguered heroine. While it should not be mistaken for an authentic or even representative expression of contemporary popular sentiment, this chorus is presented as an object of identification and sympathy for the audience: we are encouraged to side with it and to value the preservation of its 'voice', especially in the face of Nero crushing its protest. We are even encouraged, in some measure, to agree retrospectively with its assessment of the Neronian regime, thereby participating in the play's posthumous judgement of Nero. Hence, the voice of the first chorus is significant not just in acknowledging and commemorating the people's hostility towards Nero, but also in co-opting the audience's opinion and aspiring in this regard to represent the judgement of history.

It may be objected that *Octavia* also preserves Nero's voice, but the emperor's presence on stage in no way contradicts the play's remembrance of his victims. If anything, Nero's speech reinforces *Octavia*'s ideology, by allowing his full monstrosity to be articulated in the first person. Hatred of Octavia, neglect and disrespect for the state, disregard for any needs other than his own, love of tyranny and eagerness for bloodshed: all these sentiments come directly out of Nero's own mouth, preserved for posterity as proof of his despicableness. In granting Nero the opportunity to speak, the play commemorates him negatively, and in a manner far more damning than the third-personal narrative of historiography. In fact, *Octavia* allows Nero to condemn himself.

4

Language, Structure and Style

Calling *Octavia*'s author 'pseudo-Seneca' is somewhat of a misnomer, because although the play has clearly been composed within the Senecan tragic tradition, its language, dramaturgy and overall conception bear only superficial resemblance to the work of the Neronian philosopher-dramatist. *Octavia*'s vocabulary is often simpler than that of its Senecan models, its descriptions less vivid and its sentence structures more prosaic, all of which is generally assumed to indicate an inexperienced or amateur playwright. In other respects, however, *Octavia*'s author seems to deviate from Seneca deliberately, through for instance, minimalist use of proper names, or by accentuating and complicating the role of the chorus. Certainly, the play's structure is unique within extant ancient drama, and as much as this may be due to the loss of other *fabulae praetextae*, it is also evidence of a remarkably inventive dramaturgy, alert to the effects of mirror scenes, balanced action and the representation of interior space. What *Octavia* lacks in terms of poetic expression it more than compensates for in its scenic arrangement.

4.1 A shadow of Seneca

Octavia's style has rarely received good press: John Herington calls it 'clumsy' and deplores its 'flatness'; Rolando Ferri notes its pedestrian formularity, which 'betray[s] a poet less at ease in composition'.[1] Such views have a long heritage: Gustave Richter observed in the middle of the nineteenth century that 'we find that rich abundance of rhetorical style entirely lacking from this play' (*omnino . . . in hac fabula desideramus exuberantem illam . . . orationis abundantiam*).[2] Though harsh, the verdicts are not unjustified: *Octavia*'s verse makes little attempt to sparkle; no matter how independently interesting its content, the play's mode of expression remains mediocre. This feature becomes more pronounced in comparison with Senecan tragedy, for despite extensive allusions to this major dramatic predecessor, the *praetexta* fails to emulate the punchy economy of Seneca's style, its incisive phrasing and visual richness. Notably, *Octavia* employs a limited and unvarying vocabulary of generically 'tragic' words, abounding in adjectives like 'savage' (*saevus*, 33 appearances) and 'grim' (*dirus*, 20 appearances), alongside standard metaphors (e.g. 'quench with blood', *exstinguere sanguine*, *Oct.* 264, 608, 830) and cliched literary idioms (e.g. *post fata* for 'after the death of', *Oct.* 96, 112, 289, 529).[3] While such statistics should not be taken in isolation – for the Senecan dramatic corpus is too small to give a fair impression of *Octavia*'s style[4] – the play's lack of lexical variety is telling. One example will suffice: Octavia in the opening scene says of Agrippina, 'that grim Fury (*Erinys*) carried (*praetulit*) the Stygian torches (*Stygios ignes*) at my wedding (*thalamis*)' (*Oct.* 23–4). The image reappears when Octavia recollects her mother, Messalina's, illegal marriage with Silius: 'a vengeful Fury (*Erinys*) attended that Stygian (*Stygios*) union and quenched with blood the torches (*faces*) snatched from the wedding (*thalamis*)' (263–4). Next, Agrippina herself revisits the idea when promising grief, not joy, for Poppaea and Nero's union: 'I have come from Tartarus bearing (*praeferens*) in my bloodied (*cruenta*) right hand a Stygian torch (*Stygiam facem*) for this calamitous wedding (*thalamis*)' (593–5). The final iteration occurs in Poppaea's report of her dream: 'my husband's mother, fierce, with threatening mien, was shaking a torch (*facem*) stained with blood (*cruore*)' (722–3). Such repetition can, of course, be interpreted as a deliberate attempt to link these women, and (in the third instance) to reify the metaphor of Agrippina-as-Fury.[5] But the descriptions' monotony also suggests a paucity of inventive power. After all, Seneca himself uses keywords and images to interconnect specific characters and events over the course of a tragedy, for example the verb 'to follow', *sequor*, in *Thyestes*, or lexical variations on *dubitus/dubitare* – 'doubtful, hesitant, wavering, untrustworthy' – in *Oedipus*.[6] But Seneca is adroit at this technique and avoids extending it to entire cumbersome phrases.

A gulf likewise separates the two playwrights' descriptive abilities, and not only because *Octavia*'s author is less given to ekphrastic digressions.[7] Even those passages that exhibit some correspondence to Senecan tragedy are looser in design, with less attention paid to visual detail.[8] *Octavia*'s Seneca, for instance, imagines the disintegration of the universe in the following terms:

> qui si senescit,[9] tantus in caecum chaos
> casurus iterum, nunc adest mundo dies
> supremus ille, qui premat genus impium
> caeli ruina,
>
> if it is ageing, about to collapse again,
> hugely, into blind chaos, now that final day
> arrives for the world, to crush a wicked race
> with the sky's fall.
>
> *Octavia* 391–4

The passage takes its cue from the 'star chorus' of Seneca's *Thyestes*:[10]

> trepidant, trepidant pectora magno
>   percussa metu,
> ne fatali cuncta ruina
> quassata labent iterumque deos
> hominesque premat deforme chaos,
> iterum terras et mare cingens
> et uaga picti sidera mundi
>   natura tegat.

Our hearts are trembling, trembling,
    Struck by great fear
Lest everything, shaken, subside
in fatal collapse and once again
shapeless chaos crush gods and men,
again the land and encircling sea
and the wandering stars of a painted sky
    nature bury.

Thyestes 828–34

That the two passages belong to different registers is partial justification of their divergence: Seneca's is choral lyric, which encourages expressive expansion, while *Octavia*'s, in iambic trimeter, is meant to represent ordinary speech. But formal disparity is only part of the story. *Octavia*'s passage relies on mundane adjectives – *caecus* ('blind', 391); *supremus* ('final', 393); *impius* ('wicked', 393) – and includes a redundant word, *mundo* ('for the world', 392), which is already implied by context. Seneca's treatment, by contrast, applies more colourful adjectives to the standard vocabulary of cosmic conflagration: *deforme chaos* ('shapeless chaos', 832); *picti mundi* ('painted sky' 834). The chorus' fear is evoked through the well-placed repetition of *trepidant* ('they tremble') at 828 and *iterum* ('again') at 831 and 833, while postponement of the final noun/verb pairing – *natura tegat* ('nature buries', 834) – creates suspense and accentuates the atmosphere of apprehension. Conversely, the *Octavia* passage treats verbs more functionally than poetically, positioning them near the beginning of clauses – *nunc adest* ('now it arrives', 392); *qui premat* ('in order to crush', 393) – not, seemingly, to create emphasis, but out of a purely utilitarian approach to the sentence.

In keeping with this prosaic tone is *Octavia*'s oft-criticized use of disyllabic personal pronouns and possessive adjectives, especially at line ends.[11] While the practice also features in Ovid and Seneca, *Octavia*'s playwright takes it to excess, while generally disregarding – as per the descriptive passage analysed above – its potential for emphasis or poetic effect.[12] Nero's opening speech in his scene with the prefect provides a useful example:

suspecta coniunx et soror semper mihi,
tandem dolori spiritum reddat meo
iramque nostram sanguine extinguat suo.
mox tecta flammis concidant urbis meis,

let that wife and sister always mistrusted by me,
pay with her life for my anguish
and quench our anger with her blood.
Next let the city's roofs collapse in my flames.

Octavia 828–31

The position of the underlined Latin words cannot be rendered precisely into English because Latin, as an inflected language, relies less on word order. It is also more economical with pronouns – 'I', 'you', 's/he' etc. – and possessives – 'my', 'your' etc. – often omitting them when agency or ownership is implied by context (hence, while English must say, 'her life', *Octavia*'s Latin simply has *spiritum* with no possessive at 829). Latin's economy and flexibility in these respects makes *Octavia*'s practice even more striking. Many of its pronouns/possessives seem redundant – is it really necessary for Nero to say 'my flames' (*flammis … meis*) at 831? – while their overwhelming position at line ends suggests a primarily metrical purpose, namely, accommodating the short penultimate syllable required by iambic trimeter.[13] As Rolando Ferri remarks, skilled Latin poets will separate nouns from possessive adjectives for variation, elegance or effect, but *Octavia*'s author rarely bothers with such separation (e.g. *Oct.* 755: *redde te thalamis tuis*, 'return to your chamber'; or 856: *in cives tuos*, 'against your citizens').[14] The excerpt I have quoted from Nero's speech is, however, a curious example in this regard, for while a pronominal/possessive ending in four consecutive lines is undoubtedly inept, the playwright also seems to formulate, via these words, a contrast between Nero and Octavia. This is a conflict of 'she' versus 'I', 'hers' versus 'mine', and it is brought out well in line 830 where possessive adjectives are instrumental in balancing Nero's rage (*iram . . . nostram*, 'my anger') with Octavia's death (*sanguine . . . suo*, 'her blood'). For all their clumsy repetitiveness, the line endings also serve to cast Nero as stubbornly egocentric: it really is all about him. *Octavia*'s playwright is clearly capable of imbuing grammar with symbolism, so we should not assume that his/her deviation from earlier – especially Senecan – poetic standards is *always* a mark of inferiority. Sometimes the play's pragmatic, pedestrian style yields some startling results.

One such result is its avoidance of proper names. Characters in *Octavia* rarely engage in nominal identification, relying instead on an extensive yet vague lexicon of family relationships and social roles. This tactic is particularly noticeable in the opening scene, where initial, expositional speeches by Octavia and her nurse lead us to expect a cluster of proper names, but Octavia refers only to her 'mother' (Messalina, 10ff), 'stepmother' (Agrippina, 21ff) and 'father' (Claudius, 25ff). The nurse continues in the same vein, recounting how Claudius 'fell to his wife's (*coniugis*) crime, then she to her son's (*nati*), by whose poison a brother (*frater*) lies dead. The unhappy sister (*soror*) and at the same time wife (*coniunx*) . . . is compelled by her cruel husband's (*viri*) anger to hide her grief' (*Oct.* 44–8). In just five lines, the nurse covers Agrippina's poisoning of Claudius; Nero's killing of Agrippina; Nero's killing of Britannicus; Octavia's status as Nero's sister and wife (and Britannicus' sister); and Nero's status as Octavia's husband, all without mentioning a single name![15] This stylistic move represents a major departure from Senecan tragedy, in which names feature prominently: they involve etymological wordplay, are invested with talismanic power, used to parade individual reputations, measure self-worth, incite people to action, articulate solipsism and assume the magical qualities of a spell or curse.[16] Seneca's Medea is notorious for citing her own name seven times in her eponymous drama; other characters bring its usage up to fourteen. *Octavia*, by contrast, rarely mentions its heroine's name (only at 746 and 786) or patronymic (*Claudia* at 671, 789 and 803) despite its obsession with bloodlines, legitimacy and Julio-Claudian genealogy. Is this avoidance yet another symptom of the play's amateur style?

The answer is not straightforward. Eschewal of proper names may align with *Octavia*'s preference for ordinary, unadorned language. It may also be driven, partially, by the dictates of meter, because many of the longer Roman names involved in this story – e.g. 'Agrippina' and 'Messalina' – are virtually impossible to accommodate in the iambic rhythm that constitutes most of *Octavia*'s dialogue (while 'Claudia' and 'Octavia' are easier). Consequent dependence on family terms may indicate inheritance of an Ovidian – and latterly, Senecan – technique, which *Octavia*'s author deploys with less discretion and incisiveness. Both Ovid and Seneca enjoy interrogating potential conflict between social roles as restrictive facets of identity, for example, 'sister' versus 'wife' and 'mother' for Ovid's Procne, or 'wife' versus 'mother' for Seneca's Medea. But *Octavia* tends to avoid fragmenting social identities into competing components. At best, its terminology is designed to highlight the Julio-Claudians' intrafamilial conflict, and hence, the drama's fundamental tension between private desire and public duty.

If, however, *Octavia*'s naming conventions are approached as a deliberate, stylistic choice rather than an inadequacy, then other interpretations present themselves. Joseph Smith proposes that the play's relative reticence with proper names may be linked to its exploration of memory sanctions and further presupposes performance, in which any ambiguities of identification would have been resolved through mask and costume.[17] While the latter idea is untenable due to its requiring too many assumptions about staging conventions for *fabulae praetextae* – a topic about which we know almost nothing – Smith's former suggestion is fruitful, and has been elaborated by Tom Geue, who argues not just for the name's commemorative power in this play, but also for its proscriptive power, as a signal of the emperor pronouncing a death sentence.[18] From this perspective, the rare occurrence of proper names in *Octavia* is a source of significance, rather than a mere omission. Similarly, the drama's ample vocabulary of social roles becomes a means by which characters can categorize and manipulate each other's identities, so that, for instance, Agrippina is cast as archetypal stepmother and Nero as archetypal tyrant.[19] The result is fascinating interplay between the historically specific and dramatically generic, as *Octavia*'s naming strategies turn actual, historical individuals into stock characters, a tactic further compounded by the play's use of persistent stock figures such as the nurse.

General applicability of family terms also allows for slippage between roles, which *Octavia* occasionally acknowledges. In lines 45–8 of the nurse's first speech (quoted above), Octavia's designation as 'sister' relates both to the preceding image of Britannicus' death and to the heroine's ensuing definition as Nero's wife. Sisterhood for Octavia is a composite identity that has a biological foundation on the one hand and a legal foundation on the other. Consciously or not, *Octavia*'s author evokes this confusion through loose phrasing and non-specific language – features generally regarded as part of the play's stylistic failings. What this indicates, ultimately, is that the drama's supposed weaknesses do not preclude valuable thematic analysis, and that *Octavia* deserves recognition as a significant cultural and literary artefact regardless of any aesthetic deficiencies.

4.2 Dramatic technique

Of all *Octavia*'s noteworthy dramatic features, such as symmetries and mirroring, or expanded temporal scope, its chorus may not, at first, seem particularly special. Built as it is on the broad model of classical – i.e. fifth-century – Athenian tragedy, *Octavia*'s chorus adopts a traditional form, but that traditionalism is itself innovative for an early imperial Roman playwright, composing drama in an era when choral interludes were largely divorced from dramatic action. Choruses in Seneca's tragedies reflect the dominant style: they rarely interact with other characters on stage and their odes, while rich in symbolism, seldom have direct bearing on the plot.[20] In some cases, it is not even clear when the Senecan chorus enters or leaves the stage, making us uncertain as to what it has or has not overheard.[21] Such loose treatment of the chorus is characteristic of post-classical ancient drama. It can be seen developing in Greek New Comedy: surviving texts of Menander's plays have no scripted chorus, merely a note signalling their placement. The Roman comedies of Plautus and Terence have no chorus at all, and tragedy, although it preserved the choral ode, seems to have followed New Comedy in compressing its significance to the status of entr'actes.[22] Against this backdrop, *Octavia*'s citizen chorus seems remarkable for its protracted lyric accompaniment of the heroine in the play's final scene; for its knowledge of and commentary upon the play's action; and for a level of involvement that extends to direct intervention: it rebels. In formal terms, it recalls classical Athenian tragic conventions in interacting both with Octavia (899–971) and with the messenger (780–805), and in presenting itself as part of the action, for instance by acknowledging its receipt of news about the main characters (273: 'what rumour has just reached our ears?') or noting how the situation has progressed (669–72: 'look, that day . . . has dawned. Claudia has departed, banished from Nero's bed'). Its composition, too, seems reminiscent of classical Athenian models: a group of citizens deeply invested in – because deeply affected by – the events playing out on stage. Apart from *Trojan Women*, Seneca's choruses, by contrast, tend to reflect on the action without admitting much precise impact on their lives; they do not even identify themselves on first entrance, which implies the relative unimportance of their social standing and perspective on the tragedy.

Heightened choral involvement in *Octavia* may owe something to the Roman *praetexta* tradition, which, with its patriotic focus on national history and legend, presumably relied on choruses representing (subgroups of) the Roman populace. *praetextae* on military themes could have had choruses of soldiers, and there is some speculation that Accius' *Brutus* had choruses reflecting the people's divided loyalties: one for Brutus and one for Tarquin.[23] While the genre's scant remains prevent secure argument in this regard, the core hypothesis seems viable: *praetexta* choruses must have exemplified and celebrated the Roman people's active role in historical events. Certainly, *Octavia*'s choruses are designed to reflect the historical realities of popular discontent and dissent at the time of Nero's divorce, a purpose that necessitates their high degree of dramatic involvement. It seems likely, therefore, that their formal realization stems as much from the play's historical concerns as it does from models of classical Greek tragedy.

Octavia's genre, the history play, may also be responsible for the curious fact of its having not one but two choruses, a group of Roman citizens supporting Octavia and a lesser assembly of (presumably) courtiers supporting Poppaea. While not unprecedented, secondary choruses in extant ancient tragedy usually function as retinues of new and/or significant figures entering the stage: a secondary chorus of Trojan women accompanies Cassandra in Seneca's *Agamemnon* (589–781) for instance, and a chorus of religious officiants accompanies Athena in delivering the final song of Aeschylus' *Eumenides* (1003–47).[24] *Octavia* differs from this pattern in not making its secondary chorus Poppaea's retinue and in according it an importance equal to the play's primary chorus: these courtiers sing two odes and receive the messenger's speech. Such innovation produces arresting effects: it extends the play's motif of doubling and symmetry to the chorus, and it admits a diversity of popular reactions to Nero's divorce. It may even suggest different allegiances within and outside the imperial palace. While the first and main chorus, of citizen rebels, is clearly meant to command our sympathy, the inclusion of a secondary chorus implies that ideological commitment in this matter is not so clear cut. If the ancient dramatic chorus is meant to guide or in some degree represent the audience's viewpoint, then *Octavia*'s chorus all but erases the distinction between itself and the play's spectators: both represent segments of the Roman populace separated only by time. Consequently, having a double chorus is a way of prompting audiences to interrogate their political preferences, likely with the aim of their expressing compassion for Poppaea as well as Octavia.

There is also a purely functional reason for the play having two choruses, namely the messenger's reporting of Chorus 1's rebellion to . . . Chorus 2. Although the arrangement is not strictly necessary – the messenger could have delivered his news to one of the main characters instead, as happens in Seneca's *Phaedra* – the strong tradition of messenger–chorus scenes in classical Greek tragedy appears to have governed the playwright's decisions, with the result that *Octavia*'s dramaturgy balances the requirements of form with those of unavoidable historical detail. The outcome is a novel handling of dramatic convention.

It remains to consider the ancient chorus' main task of dividing plays into scenes/acts/episodes. Scholarly consensus maintains that the five-act structure typically used by Senecan tragedy is, like the chorus' increasing marginalization, a post-classical dramatic development for which the earliest extant evidence is Greek New Comedy.[25] In this schema, the standard arrangement of early imperial Roman tragedy is presumed (by extrapolation from Seneca) to entail five acts separated by four choruses with a concluding choral ode to wrap up the play's action. *Octavia*'s division is not so clear: the first chorus at 273–376 marks the end of Act 1 (Octavia and nurse), but where we might expect a second chorus between the Seneca–Nero scene (377–592) and Agrippina's ghost (593–645) none appears, despite an implied break in the play's action and a shift in time from the first to second day. The chorus' subsequent movements are just as puzzling: a brief ode (669–89) following Octavia's warnings against rebellion seems to initiate a new act (3 or 4?), while the equally brief choral ode in praise of Poppaea's beauty (762–79) functions as prelude to the chorus' exchange with the messenger, an event typically situated in Act 4. Another ode concludes the messenger–chorus scene (806–19), presumably signalling the new act between Nero and the prefect. An ode likewise follows this exchange (877–98), before leading into the final scene of the chorus accompanying Octavia in lament. The chorus remains alone on stage to bring the play to an end at 972–82.

A conservative estimate grants *Octavia* six acts, which is not unreasonable given the concomitant example of Seneca's *Oedipus*, but does not account for the apparent pause between 592 and 593.[26] Proposals that accommodate this pause extend the play's acts to seven,[27] an arrangement unparalleled in extant ancient drama and bordering on disarray. Disparities in the length of scenes, and the truncation of choral odes in the latter half of the play, suggest uneven composition; lines 273–376 is *Octavia*'s only substantial choral song of the kind used for act divisions in Senecan tragedy. The schema of acts is indeed so loose in *Octavia* that it does not appear to have been the playwright's primary method of arranging dramatic material.

An alternative and more profitable structuring principle is the three-day span of *Octavia*'s action. Day 1 comprises the Octavia–nurse and Seneca–Nero scenes, as well as the first choral ode; Day 2 opens with Agrippina' ghost, followed by Octavia and the chorus; Day 3 features the Poppaea–nurse, chorus–messenger and Nero–prefect scenes, and ends with Octavia's departure. Content is still uneven, with Day 3 comprising a disproportionate number of shorter scenes,[28] but the playwright's desire for symmetry is obvious. I have noted already in Chapter 3 ('Symmetries') the play's essentially dyadic structure that divides action into 'before' and 'after' the pivotal event of Nero and Poppaea's wedding. Day 1 illustrates anticipation of the event and various characters' attempts to forestall it. Day 3 represents the aftermath: civic rebellion; Octavia's exile; and a lingering sense of Poppaea's grim future. Ellipsis of the wedding itself is a striking feature of Day 2: the ceremony is anticipated by Agrippina (594–6) and completed prior to Octavia's subsequent entry (646), a manipulation of time that may seem heavy-handed but actually succeeds in presenting Day 2, likewise, as a dyad of 'before' and 'after'. The drama's second day is designed in such a way that it becomes a central, condensed version of *Octavia*'s overall structure.

Octavia herself provides dramatic unity in being the only character to appear on each of these three days.[29] The two other imperial women, Agrippina and Poppaea, feature on Days 2 and 3 respectively, and are linked via their mutual evocations of the underworld. Nero makes balanced appearances on Days 1 and 3 in scenes clearly designed to resemble each other. Standard pairings – nurse and noblewoman; rule and advisor – are interwoven in the formula *abab* and represent gendered equivalents of the conventional persuasion scene, such that a version of Octavia's resistance to her nurse is replayed in Nero's resistance to Seneca, while Poppaea's nurse and Nero's prefect resemble each other in their endeavour to guide powerful superiors. All *Octavia*'s dialogue scenes adhere to a strict principle of one or two speaking characters, with most scenes relying on a combination of one dominant and one lesser/weaker individual, divided according to status: Octavia (dominant) versus nurse (lesser); Seneca (lesser) versus Nero (dominant); prefect (lesser) versus Nero (dominant). The only mild exception is the Poppaea–nurse exchange, which, while clearly a pairing of superior and inferior, does not share other scenes' antagonism.

Besides her appearance on each of the drama's three days, Octavia's prominence is further confirmed through her close relationship with the chorus. She is the only character to interact with the chorus apart from the messenger, and his role is more customary than expressive of specific rapport. Octavia by contrast speaks directly to the Roman populace at 646–50, warning them to avoid demonstrations of partisanship in the wake of Nero's divorce, and joins them in mourning her departure from Rome at 899–971. Her exclusive interaction with the first of the play's two choral groups not only corresponds to the historical reality of Romans rioting in support of Octavia, but also directs audience sympathies towards her as the main recipient of collective loyalty.

Octavia's contact with the chorus also depends upon the play's representation of interior and exterior space: where precisely does she interact with the *populus*, and can we chart her movements inside and outside the palace? The play's spatial arrangement is a topic of some disagreement. Rolando Ferri, for instance, situates Octavia's opening monody (1–33) outside the palace, arguing from the playwright's imitation of Sophocles' *Electra* that this song must occur outdoors. But the hypothesis is implausible, and it requires Ferri to reposition Octavia *inside* the palace to fit the nurse's comments at 72–4 – an awkward, unmotivated move that he attributes to the playwright's subsequent evocation of Euripides' *Medea*.[30] Similar uncertainty colours his evaluation of the Poppaea–nurse scene,[31] in which Poppaea is described as rushing out from Nero's bedchamber to an undisclosed location (690–1): where does her conversation with the nurse take place?

While Ferri's concerns are valid and *Octavia*'s opening scene is particularly unclear about the heroine's movements, I prefer Joseph Smith's schema, in which Octavia delivers her initial monody from 'inside' her chamber (after all, she does not have to imitate Electra comprehensively, and she can describe dawn's arrival (1–4) just as well from a window as from outside).[32] Stage space therefore represents the palace's interior. Moreover, Octavia does not have to exit the stage before the nurse's entry at 34 but merely draw aside to a far corner before advancing toward the centre again, gradually, in the nurse's company at 75ff. The nurse is imagined standing 'outside' Octavia's chamber in another area of the stage. This seems the easiest solution. There is no reason to apply classical Athenian conventions of entrance and exit to this scene, nor to assume a Greek use of the 'moveable platform' (*ekkyklema*) to symbolize disclosure of interior space at 75ff, as Anthony Boyle does.[33] *Octavia*'s dramaturgy already exhibits too many post-classical elements to warrant being fitted to the contours of fifth-century BCE tragedy, and precedent for two characters being on stage without fully acknowledging each other's presence is well established prior to *Octavia*, by Roman comedy and Senecan tragedy. The post-classical and especially Roman stage enjoyed greater flexibility in its handling of dramatic space and time.[34] *Octavia* belongs to this later tradition, with the result that it can effectively suspend one character's activity to focus on another's, or have the stage represent distinct (albeit in this case adjacent) localities in quick succession. It can also have the stage serve as interior space for most of the play.

Such concentration on private, domestic space is another of *Octavia*'s dramaturgical singularities, for no other extant ancient drama situates so much of its action indoors. Both classical Athenian drama and Greek/Roman traditions of New Comedy maintain the pretence that stage space represents outdoors, with interior activity being communicated to the audience via noises off, or the appearance of a moveable platform. Senecan tragedy differs in occasionally presenting interior scenes directly before the audience (e.g. *Thyestes* 885–919, where Atreus must be inside already, prior to the additional disclosure of Thyestes' internal location, at the feast). *Octavia*, however, envisages its story occurring predominantly within the oppressive confines of the imperial palace: the scene between Octavia and her nurse takes place primarily within the former's chamber; Seneca's encounter with Nero is likewise imagined as happening indoors, in a separate part of the palace; Poppaea and her nurse conduct their exchange inside, not far from the threshold of Nero's chamber; the chorus of courtiers most likely receives the messenger's report indoors; and Nero's exchange with the prefect happens inside, too. Agrippina's ghost may seem to occupy a nebulous pre-dawn realm not explicitly defined as interior or exterior, but there is good reason to situate her, too, within the palace, because of her express intent to participate in Nero and Poppaea's wedding ceremony (594–6) and because her disruption of the household is modelled on Tantalus' entry into and disturbance of the domestic sphere in Seneca's *Thyestes* (*Thy.* 83–6; 101–5). The only of *Octavia*'s scenes indisputably occurring outdoors are the choral odes performed by the populace (i.e. Chorus 1), Octavia's departure from the palace and brief address to the chorus following the wedding (646–68) and her distraught removal from Rome at the drama's end.

The result is visual enactment of Octavia's expulsion. The play's dramaturgy illustrates her changing status from wife, to ex-wife, to exile – a transition emphasized by her movement from inside to outside the palace. Particularly effective in this regard is the scene shift at 689–90, where Octavia has left the palace and the audience's attention is returned inside, to witness the Poppaea–nurse dialogue. This allows the audience to accomplish what Octavia cannot: it can re-enter the palace and resume involvement in the imperial family's domestic narrative. The shift also underscores Poppaea's replacement of Octavia, not just because she occupies an equivalent scene – as I have already discussed in Chapter 3 ('Symmetries') – but because she is now the focal female occupant of interior space, a visual indication of her establishment as Nero's new wife.

The relationship between the worlds inside and outside the palace is therefore a key factor in *Octavia*'s scenic arrangement. Even the play's two choruses appear to be divided along these lines, with the first, pro-Octavia group consistently occupying exterior space while the second, pro-regime group, never leaves the palace. Dramaturgy illuminates the gulf in their perspectives and status. Further, as Joseph Smith has shown, interior space in *Octavia* is often threatened and violated by incursions from outside, whether imagined (in the form of Octavia's and Poppaea's dreams), otherworldly (Agrippina's ghost) or frighteningly real (the chorus' attempt to storm the palace and abduct Poppaea).[35] Repeated images of intrusion articulate, in miniature, the central, historical event of popular insurrection. They also imply that living inside the palace is no guarantee of protection, either from external assaults such as citizen violence or internal ones such as the emperor's displeasure. After all, Nero is the one responsible for displacing Octavia from her family home (665–8), and both Octavia's and Poppaea's dreams conclude with his violent entry and infliction of presumably fatal stab wounds (121–2; 732–3): Nero is clearly presented as the enemy within. And just as Nero effects Octavia's movement from inside to outside the imperial residence, so the citizen body, in the form of the first choral group, tries to gain entry: *Octavia*'s dramaturgy presents them as equal and opposite actions. Nero's alienation from his people, and from Rome, is cleverly encapsulated by *Octavia*'s strategic scenic arrangement – its superb, unparalleled portrayal of interior and exterior space.

5

Reception

Octavia's influence post antiquity is remarkable: widespread yet coherent, and disproportionate to the play's significance in its original Roman context. While few Roman authors appear to have been inspired by or adapted *Octavia*'s material,[1] the play later becomes a crucial source for early Humanist, Renaissance and Early Modern drama, and for a long-lived tradition of operas about Nero. It is, in Gesine Manuwald's words 'the typological ancestor and starting point for all plays on historical subjects in the tradition of European theatre'.[2] Similarly, its prominent themes of love and marriage allow for an easy transition into the romantic world of opera and are probably the main reason for the play attracting continued attention from composers and librettists. *Octavia*'s mixed and multilayered genre, which poses such a challenge to classical scholarship, is a significant strength in the context of its later appropriation, as it enables this chameleon work to blend into different forms of performance.

5.1 Renaissance and Early Modern drama

The story of *Octavia*'s literary afterlife begins in early fourteenth-century Italy with Albertino Mussato, a statesman, historian and playwright whose writings catalysed the development of Renaissance Humanism. Often called a pre- or protohumanist, Mussato was well-versed in classical Latin literature and instrumental in its revival. His Senecan-inflected *Ecerinis* (1314) was the first secular tragedy composed since antiquity and a major source of inspiration for tragic and historical drama during the Renaissance. *Octavia* is one of the play's main dramatic ancestors, exercising broad influence over Mussato's form and content despite only minor instances of verbal borrowing.

A summary of *Ecerinis*' plot is necessary to understanding the quality and extent of *Octavia*'s influence. Mussato's tragedy charts the rise and fall of the historical tyrant Ezzelino III da Romano (AKA Ecerinus), whose battles and expansionist ambitions it depicts episodically, as a selection of five critical days occurring over the span of Ezzelino's career, from 1223 to 1259.[3] The play begins with Ezzelino's mother, Adeleita, telling Ezzelino and his brother, Alberico, that she conceived them when raped by the devil. Ezzelino receives the tale as proof of his greatness and authorization of his violent desires. He invokes his father, Lucifer, to guarantee his criminal aspirations. Exit Ezzelino; enter a chorus lamenting the deadly consequences of ambition and jealousy. It wonders at the present uproar in Padua, Treviso, Vincenza and Verona, until a messenger arrives to report that Ezzelino has taken these territories in the wake of civil unrest. Alone once more, the chorus calls for God's intervention before proceeding to recount Ezzelino's cruelty against innocent Paduans: he has babies mutilated and women's breasts cut off. Act 3 opens with Ezzelino boasting of his triumphs and encouraging his brother to match his imperialist aggression. The next scene takes us to Mantua, where Ezzelino's half-brother, Ziramonte, reports the city's capitulation; Ezzelino reacts by calling joyously for indiscriminate slaughter, and when Friar Luca attempts to curb his violence, advising mercy and repentance, Ezzelino easily outsmarts the priest's arguments to conclude that he is in fact God's instrument, a scourge for mankind on the model of the Old Testament. The following scene has a messenger report to Ezzelino that Padua has been retaken; Ezzelino commands his soldiers to march there at once. The chorus arrives and tells of Ezzelino's unsuccessful attempt to repossess the city; enraged, he returns to Verona to slaughter thousands of Paduan prisoners. Act 4 sees Ezzelino planning to conquer Lombardy before the scene shifts to an exchange between a messenger and the chorus: Ezzelino has been killed during his attack on Milan; the chorus gives thanks. The exchange continues into Act 5, which represents the tragedy's bloody epilogue: the messenger reports, in brutal detail, the murder/ execution of Alberico, Ezzelino's brother, along with his wife and children, at the hands of an avenging army from Treviso, Vincenza and Padua. The chorus is satisfied that justice has been done.

Ecerinis' experimental form combines Seneca's tragedies with the pseudo-Senecan *Octavia*. Like *Octavia*'s Nero, Ezzelino is a tyrant on the model of Seneca's Atreus: he is clever, blatantly amoral, rejoices in violence and expresses dissatisfaction with the extent of his own criminality (*Ec.* 295–7; 457). The play also acknowledges its connection to *Octavia* via two direct references to Nero: the chorus in Act 2 declares that Ezzelino's brutality outstrips Nero's (*Ec.* 246), and Ezzelino himself praises 'Nero of happy memory' (*felicis . . . memoriae . . . Nero*, *Ec.* 393) as a model for his tyrannous pursuits, a metapoetic allusion that recognizes Ezzelino's and *Ecerinis*' literary prototype. Further links to *Octavia* include *Ecerinis*' citizen chorus;[4] its celebration of political freedom and overt support for popular rebellion; and its grafting of historical subject matter onto the framework of tragedy. Mussato's *Ecerinis* resembles *Octavia* in portraying a period of (relatively) recent history, concentrating attention on its grimmest aspects and allowing historical optimism to emerge implicitly from the central villain's guaranteed demise. *Ecerinis* is more heavy-handed than *Octavia* in this regard because it provides a full account of Ezzelino's and Alberico's bloody ends, whereas the ancient play merely hints at Nero's ruin and leaves the audience to draw its own conclusions. Finally, both dramas adopt a patriotic stance in their criticism of autocratic incursion: *Octavia* celebrates Rome and *Ecerinis* Padua. Mussato's tragedy was in fact so well received in his native city that it earned him a laurel crown, and was recited annually, in the town hall and the author's presence, as a means of strengthening civic pride.[5]

Mussato's most overt imitation of *Octavia* occurs in Act 3, which features a confrontation between Ezzelino and the advisory figure of Friar Luca. The latter character is clearly based on *Octavia*'s Seneca: he intervenes to counsel self-restraint at a moment when Ezzelino is planning violent reprisals, and Ezzelino, like *Octavia*'s Nero, reacts to him with a mixture of impatience and disdain. The friar espouses Christian precepts in place of Seneca's Stoic morality and echoes the Neronian philosopher in his brief opening description of celestial bodies orbiting the heavens (*Ec.* 350–4; *Oct.* 387–90). *Ecerinis* and *Octavia* exhibit similar dramaturgy here as well, since both exchanges end with the counsellor's rhetorical defeat yet deftly reinforce his authority by using the immediately following scene to predict a reversal in the tyrant's fortunes. In *Octavia*, Nero trumps Seneca's arguments, but the ensuing scene in which Agrippina's ghost prophecies his downfall indicates that his victory will be short-lived, and that moral supremacy actually lies with Seneca. *Ecerinis* performs an equivalent trick by juxtaposing Ezzelino's dismissive treatment of Friar Luca (*Ec.* 367–97) with a messenger's report of Paduan exiles recapturing the previously conquered city (*Ec.* 398–411). This is the beginning of Ezzelino's demise, and it implicitly vindicates the friar's viewpoint: Ezzelino deserves and will receive punishment, just like *Octavia*'s Nero, regardless of the force of his rhetoric.

After Mussato, this counsellor–tyrant scene becomes a standard feature of subsequent tragedies in the *Octavia* tradition, due in part to *Ecerinis*' popularity, but principally to its being *Octavia*'s strongest and most deeply Senecan piece of dramatic action. Seneca claimed considerable cultural cachet during the Renaissance, especially in the period's early Italian phases, when the texts of Greek tragedy had not yet entered wide circulation,[6] and when Seneca's political philosophy,

On Clemency in particular, was celebrated and imitated.[7] The Seneca–Nero exchange in *Octavia* represents the intersection of these two cultural vectors because it is modelled on Senecan tragedy (Atreus and his minister at *Thyestes* 176–335) *and* uses *On Clemency* as a key intertext. The combination proved irresistible to numerous pre- and early Italian Renaissance dramatists, including Leonardo Dati, whose historical drama, *Hiempsal* (1440s), draws on both *Thyestes* and *On Clemency* for its counsellor–tyrant scene (*Hiem.* 173–219), and more famously, Giambattistia Giraldi Cinzio, who combined the two Senecan texts in his *Orbecche* (1541). The latter of these two works deserves full consideration, not just for its reworking of the counsellor–tyrant scene, but also for its broader recasting of material from *Octavia*.

Cinzio's *Orbecche* is a landmark text that embodies a new model of theatrical technique and leaves behind a substantial theatrical legacy.[8] An early example of *tragedia regolare* ('standard tragedy'), *Orbecche* was composed according to neoclassical dramatic conventions and intended specifically for performance (whereas earlier plays, like Mussato's *Ecerinis*, were designed to be recited).[9] Cinzio followed Mussato in being a learned Latinist who clearly knew ancient texts like *Octavia* and *Thyestes* first-hand, as demonstrated by *Orbecche*'s creative engagement with them. He was, in addition, well acquainted with Greek tragedy – *Orbecche* makes use of Sophocles' *Electra* – and claimed an abiding interest in the theory as well as practice of playwrighting, best illustrated in his *Discourse on Tragedy and Comedy*, published in 1543, the same year *Orbecche* appeared in print. The play marks a turning point in *Octavia*'s dramatic adaptation, building on Mussato's foundations while also exhibiting a greater degree of theatrical intricacy and self-awareness.

As noted above, *Orbecche* combines material from Seneca's *Thyestes* and the pseudo-Senecan *Octavia*, the most obvious debts to which are apparent from the plot. The tragedy tells the story of Orbecche, daughter of Sulmone, the king of Persia. Orbecche has married Oronte without her father's knowledge; the couple have two children. But now Sulmone has decided to marry his daughter to a neighbouring potentate, and Orbecche bewails her fate. She enlists the help of the king's minister, Malecche, who tries to persuade Sulmone to forgive the couple. Sulmone pretends to have been persuaded and invites Oronte to the palace along with the two children, on the pretext of reconciliation and celebration of the couple's marriage. Oronte is slaughtered, his hands and head cut off and retained while his body is thrown to the beasts; the children are stabbed and arranged on a platter for Orbecche to unveil, daggers still buried in their bodies. Distraught at the unveiling, Orbecche seizes a dagger and murders her father before committing suicide in the final scene. It is not hard to see Seneca's *Thyestes* here. Sulmone is an Atrean figure: amoral, tyrannical, cunning, brutal, concerned about the purity of the family's bloodline and avenging himself against the offending party by killing her children in the context of a fictitious celebration. He quotes Atreus extensively in his monologue in Act 3, Scene 3 (668–748),[10] and clearly aspires to Atreus' model of absolute, unaccountable rulership.[11] Seneca's *Thyestes* is also a major source for the encounter between Malecche and Sulmone (3.2.89–667), while Sulmone's unveiling of Oronte and the children's remains in Act 5 owes as much to Atreus' grisly revelation (*Thy.* 1004–5, where the children's hands and heads have been preserved – cf. *Thy.* 764) as it does to Orestes uncovering the dead Clytemnestra before Aegisthus in Sophocles' *Electra* (1474–6).

Accompanying this pervasive use of *Thyestes* is the equally pervasive use of *Octavia*. Notably, Cinzio's *Orbecche* follows *Octavia* in pivoting upon the issue of marriage to a new spouse who does not have the support of the populace (Poppaea in *Octavia* and Selim, king of the Parthians, in *Orbecche*). Orbecche herself resembles Octavia in fearing a tyrannous ruler's treatment of her and lamenting his prior aggression against other family members (e.g. *Orb.* 2.3.360–6). Like Octavia,

Orbecche cannot forget that her father murdered her mother, Selina, for sexual indiscretion; in both plays, intrafamilial violence directs the action like a curse. Orbecche's first appearance also reworks *Octavia*'s opening scene, in which the heroine cries inconsolably about her current circumstances while a nurse tries to calm her anxieties and advise a more positive outlook (*Orb.* 2.1). Other allusions to *Octavia* include Selina's ghost, who, like Agrippina's, prophecies the tyrant Sulmone's death (*Orb.* 1.2.139–71) and Orbecche's foreboding dream (*Orb.* 5.2.183–216), which, like Poppaea's in *Octavia*, visits her in an ostensibly celebratory context. The tragedy's focus on female characters may also reflect *Octavia*'s predominantly female cast and female view of history.[12] Even *Orbecche*'s chief Greek tragic intertext, Sophocles' *Electra*, is a likely link to *Octavia*, for it is the ancient Roman play's main Greek intertext as well.

As in *Ecerinis*, *Octavia*'s influence is felt most powerfully in *Orbecche*'s counsellor–tyrant scene, which occupies the first half of Act 3. Replicating *Octavia*'s dramaturgy, the encounter begins with Malecche, in a quasi-Senecan role, delivering a monologue before the ruler enters (*Orb.* 3.1). When Sulmone arrives, Malecche advises the king to show clemency to his daughter and newly discovered son-in-law. The counsellor's arguments are a pastiche of Seneca's *On Clemency* and *Moral Letters*; Cinzio signals the texts' presence by having Malecche assert that, 'there are few people who know how to endure misfortune wisely' (*ma pochi son, che la fortuna aversa / sappiano tolerar prudentemente*, *Orb.* 3.2.173–4). A steady stream of Senecan advice ensues: pardoning is a virtue most suited to sovereigns (*Orb.* 3.2.185–6; cf. *Clemency* 1.3.3); self-restraint is the greatest empire for a king (*Orb.* 3.2.210–13; cf. *Letters* 113.30); and displays of virtue can only elevate a king's standing and clemency equates men to gods (*Orb.* 3.2.240–52 and 273; cf. *Clemency* 1.5.2–7). In echo of *Octavia*'s Nero (583), Sulmone protests that forgiveness would constitute a diminution of his power (*Orb.* 3.2.194–7); he wants to show Orbecche and Oronte 'what sceptres and crowns can do' (*ciò che possano gli scettri, et le corone, Orb.* 3.2.200), a sentiment that sounds distinctly Atrean, both in its impersonal form and its equation of power with violence.

The scene is a prime example of *Orbecche*'s complex debt to *Octavia*. First, it follows the *praetexta* in modelling its tyrant on Seneca's Atreus (in fact, Sulmone is an admixture of Atreus and Nero), and second, it uses the counsellor figure to evoke the historical Seneca, primarily through citation of Seneca's own philosophy. This combination demonstrates that Cinzio understood *Octavia*'s dual reception of Seneca's *Thyestes* and his prose works, and further understood how *Octavia* interrogates the Senecan tragic paradigm of tyranny.[13] Just as the *praetexta* reminds its audience of Nero's eventual overthrow, so *Orbecche* ensures Sulmone's defeat – and this time there is the added satisfaction of our witnessing the tyrant's death on stage (*Orb.* 5.3.387–404).

Having taken root at the very beginnings of Renaissance drama, the joint reception of *Thyestes* and *Octavia* spread from Italy across Europe: adaptations like those already discussed are found in English, French and Spanish traditions as well.[14] If, moreover, Gordon Braden is correct in asserting that 'the history of every major national theatre in the Renaissance includes an early phase . . . of formal Senecan imitation',[15] then *Octavia*'s popularity in that period might be due, in part, to its status as an adjunct member of the Senecan corpus. Regardless of opinions about its authorship – by the sixteenth century, few believed it was written by Seneca[16] – *Octavia*'s transmission alongside Seneca's genuine works, and its inventive appropriation of Senecan language and motifs, enabled it to ride the wave of Senecan admiration and secure an adjacent place in the Roman dramatic canon. Yet its influence was also more multifaceted than mere Senecanism, and its value as the prototype of a history play should not be ignored. Interestingly, imitation of *Octavia* often occurs at the inception of national dramatic traditions, when playwrights look to it as a model of patriotic theatre:

it is the touchstone for Mussato's dramatization of history in *Ecerinis*, and likewise for Sackville and Norton's *Gorboduc* (1561), the first secular verse drama in English, which enacts a quasi-legendary tale from early English history. In fact, *Gorboduc*'s handling of *Octavia* derives equally from the *praetexta*'s Senecan qualities and historical subject matter. As a story of two brothers, Ferrex and Porrex, vying for control of their father Gorboduc's kingdom, *Gorboduc* adapts motifs from Seneca's *Thyestes*, including a double version of the much-imitated counsellor–tyrant scene, involving not just one but two advisers on each occasion (*Gorb.* 2.1.463–675 and 2.2.676–757).[17] At the same time, the play's historical interrogation of tyranny, and its setting a tale of royal conflict against a backdrop of popular dissent, points to the influence of *Octavia*. *Gorboduc* even signals *Octavia*'s presence in its opening scene, when Videna, the queen, and mother of Ferrex and Porrex, laments that with the coming of dawn, 'the day renews my griefull plaint' (*Gorb.* 1.1.6). Although verbal echoes such as this are few, *Gorboduc*'s blending of Senecan tragedy with national history, alongside its historical recasting of the counsellor–tyrant exchange, indicates the authors' strong knowledge and innovative treatment of the pseudo-Senecan *Octavia*.

Following *Gorboduc*'s lead and the trends established by Italian Humanism, English Renaissance tragedy recognizes the significance of *Octavia*'s compound genre, specifically its historicizing view of Seneca. The *praetexta*'s combination of tragic themes and historical setting inspires to various degrees a broad group of dramatists from Edwards (*Damon and Pithias*, 1567) to Shakespeare (*King Lear*, 1605–6).[18] Its role as a model of nationally inflected drama peaks with Thomas Hughes's *The Misfortunes of Arthur* (1587), while its adaptation of Senecan aesthetics features prominently in John Marston's *Antonio's Revenge* (1599–1600). It is to these two plays that I now turn, as representative examples of *Octavia*'s converging themes and their reception by late sixteenth-century English theatre.

Like *Gorboduc*, *The Misfortunes of Arthur* grafts a tragic plot onto quasi-legendary subject matter. The play begins with the ghost of Gorlois, erstwhile Duke of Cornwall, swearing revenge for his murder by Arthur's father, Uther Pendragon. In a manner reminiscent of *Thyestes*' Fury (23–67), Gorlois calls for successive feats of surpassing criminality (*Misfor. Ar.* 1.1.18–26) and summarizes the play's events in the context of intrafamilial murder. The ensuing scenes reveal that King Arthur is absent from Britain on a military expedition against the Romans and his wife Guenevera is locked in a love affair with Mordred, his illegitimate son. Mordred is ambitious, power-hungry and unscrupulous; despite his counsellor Conan's attempts at dissuasion, he plots to ambush Arthur on his return. When the ambush fails and Arthur extends an offer of reconciliation, Mordred opts instead to face his father in battle. They meet in single combat and Arthur kills Mordred while himself sustaining a mortal wound. The final scenes present Arthur's dying requests, Gorlois' satisfied ghost and an epilogue in praise of virtue as the route to everlasting renown.

The play overall is an unremitting pastiche of Senecan and pseudo-Senecan tragedy, with some of Lucan's *Civil War* thrown in for good measure.[19] Hughes's borrowings are sometimes judicious (he uses Seneca's Phaedra and Clytemnestra for the portrait of Guenevera) and sometimes random in their attribution and effects (in Act 1, Scenes 2 and 3, Guenevera also echoes Oedipus, Medea and Octavia in quick succession). While it can be difficult to detect a coherent pattern in this use of Senecan material, or to ascribe it a single distinct purpose, isolated episodes reveal Hughes's subtle, innovative engagement with his dramatic sources, especially his understanding of *Octavia*'s relationship to Seneca's *Thyestes*. A particularly telling example is the first encounter between Mordred and his advisor, Conan, which is another variation on the counsellor–tyrant scene. Mordred is bent on attacking Arthur while Conan cautions him against acquiring a reputation for brutality:

Conan: But think what fame and grievous bruits would run
Of such disloyal and unjust attempts.

Mordred: Fame goes not with our ghosts: the senseless soul,
Once gone, neglects what vulgar bruit reports.
She is both light and vain.

Conan: She noteth, though.

Mordred: She feareth states.

Conan: She carpeth, ne'ertheless.

Mordred: She's soon suppress'd.

Conan: As soon she springs again.
Tongues are untam'd and fame is envy's dog,
That absent barks, and present fawns as fast.
It fearing dares, and yet hath never done,
But dures: though death redeem us all from foes
Besides, yet death redeems us not from tongues.

The Misfortunes of Arthur, 1.4.117–28

The blueprint for this exchange is *Thyestes* 204–7, where the minister warns Atreus about the power of hostile rumours and Atreus dismisses them as being beneath the power of a king. The issue resurfaces at *Octavia* 583–6, with the roles reversed: Nero worries about appearing weak and Seneca, in true Stoic mode, brushes this off as an insubstantial threat. Hughes combines the two sources, making Mordred resemble Seneca's Atreus in his unconcern for 'what vulgar bruit reports' (*Misf. Ar.* 1.4.120), yet basing the characters' stichomythia on *Octavia* 583–6, which he translates almost verbatim.[20] The result is a complex 'window' reference accompanied by *oppositio in imitando*: Hughes shows how *Octavia* changes *Thyestes*, first by expanding the topic of debate, then by exchanging the speakers' positions, so that the tyrant expresses anxiety over not seeming sufficiently autocratic instead of the minister reminding him to beware of gaining a bad reputation. It is as though *Octavia*'s Nero is aware of not quite being Atreus: he aspires to but falls short of Atreus' self-confident dismissiveness.

Further, Hughes's adaptation of the scene acknowledges and builds upon *Octavia*'s historical perspective, by associating Mordred's 'fame' with the judgement of history and hence, implicitly, the judgement of the play itself. By linking the characters' immediate discussion of personal renown to broader issues of historical commemoration, Hughes not only recognizes the role played by historical drama in forming reputations and preserving memories, but also, more specifically, *Octavia*'s role in presenting and aspiring to perpetuate a negative assessment of Nero. Nero's *fama* (*Oct.* 583), like Mordred's, encompasses both present and future: it is his immediate reputation with the Roman people – the subject of this part of his debate with Seneca – *and* his posthumous representation, created in part by the play itself. Each drama's historical frame allows us to see that the tyrant figure points his energies in the wrong direction: Mordred seems a fool for according posthumous renown no importance, and Nero for wanting his severity celebrated. In drawing out this latent element of *Octavia* 583–6, Hughes proves himself an astute interpreter of the *praetexta*'s main themes.

The Misfortunes of Arthur and *Gorboduc* join *Ecerinis* in transporting *Octavia* to the world of masculine enterprise, in contrast to Cinzio's *Orbecche*, which foregrounds female agency. In part, this is due to the former plays' historical focus, where men featured more prominently,[21] and to *Orbecche*'s fuller imitation of ancient – i.e. Roman *and Greek* – tragedy, which traditionally granted women more airtime. The development highlights, incidentally, just how innovative *Octavia* is in portraying Nero's reign through a prism of female voices. The innovation, however, is rarely maintained by later playwrights, especially in the English tradition, where Senecanism tends to mean violence, forceful rhetoric and hypermasculine behaviour. This may be yet another reason for the perpetuation of

Octavia's counsellor–tyrant scene: it is male-centric, as well as being the *praetexta*'s most Senecan episode.

This association of Senecan style and masculine force is brought out clearly in John Marston's *Antonio's Revenge* (1599–1600), in which the central figure of Piero Sforza, Duke of Venice, resembles Seneca's Atreus. The play begins with Piero having murdered his love rival, Andrugio, under pretence of reconciliation, as well as having stabbed Feliche, son of the courtier Pandulpho, and suspended the young man's body in his daughter, Mellida's, chamber. By these acts, Piero hopes to marry Andrugio's widow, Maria, whom he has long desired, and to drive a rift between Mellida and her fiancé Antonio, the dead Andrugio's son. Mellida alerts Antonio to her father's plotting; Antonio adopts a disguise to prepare revenge against the duke. Mellida dies upon hearing a false report of Antonio's death, but Piero presses on regardless with his own marriage celebrations. A masque is prepared for Piero and Maria's entertainment. After the performance, Piero dismisses his courtiers and remains alone with the masquers, who reveal themselves as Antonio, Pandulpho and other avenging company. They bind Piero, tear out his tongue and present him with his own son's mutilated remains before killing him. Andrugio's ghost rejoices and the avengers, after being congratulated by the Venetian Senate, withdraw to spend the rest of their lives in a monastery.

Piero's Atrean characterization is apparent in his violent disdain for common morality and pursuit of unfettered autocratic power. In fact, he is a blend of Seneca's Atreus and *Octavia*'s Nero, as Marston makes clear by having Andrugio's ghost echo, in Latin, Agrippina's promise of future retribution against Nero: *venit dies, tempusque, quo reddat suis / animam squallentum sceleribus* ('the day and time has come when he renders up his foul soul in payment for his crimes' *Ant. Rev.* 5.1.1–2; cf. *Oct.* 629–30, with *nocentem* rather than *squallentum*). Just as Agrippina foresees Nero's demise, so Andrugio anticipates Piero's. The quotation highlights *Octavia*'s little recognized status as a version of revenge drama, one in which retaliation against the central villain has already been guaranteed by history.[22] Marston follows *Octavia* in ensuring the play's Atrean figure receives his comeuppance, a fate the original Atreus never suffers in *Thyestes*.[23] This shift in power is particularly brutal in *Antonio's Revenge*, with Piero moving from Atrean supremacy to being a version of Thyestes in the final scenes, where, a helpless victim, he is presented with his son's remains as – metaphorically – 'a dish to feast thy father's gorge' (*Ant. Rev.* 5.5.50).[24]

A closer example of overlap between *Thyestes* and *Octavia* occurs in Act 2, Scene 2 of Marston's tragedy, when an encounter between Piero and the courtier Pandulpho morphs into a debate on the nature of kingship. Pandulpho adopts Seneca's role from *Octavia*, an affinity reinforced by his being labelled a 'stoic gentleman' in the play's list of characters. Piero responds to Pandulpho's caveats by channelling Atreus/Nero in his contempt for virtue and populism. In echo of *Octavia* 459, Piero proclaims, ''Tis just that subjects act commands of kings,' to which Pandulpho replies 'command then just and honourable things' (*Ant. Rev.* 2.2.53–4). The duke's next assertion – 'where only honest deeds to kings are free / it is no empire but a beggary' (*Ant. Rev.* 2.2.57–8) – reworks Atreus' at *Thyestes* 214–15 ('wherever a sovereign is permitted only honourable things, he rules on sufferance', *ubicumque tantum honesta dominanti licent, / precario regnatur*) and he continues in this Atrean vein for much of the debate: subjects must not just bear but praise their ruler's actions (*Ant. Rev.* 2.2.62–3; cf. *Thy.* 205–7) and receiving false praise is a mark of true power (*Ant. Rev.* 2.2.66–7; cf. *Thy.* 211–12). His dismissal of Pandulpho as a 'juiceless greybeard' (*Ant. Rev.* 2.2.61) and 'doting Stoic' (2.2.71) alludes to Nero's youthful contempt for Seneca's age and pedagogical role at *Octavia* 445 ('a soft old man should be instructing boys', *praecipere mitem convenit pueris senem*), while Pandulpho's remark, ''Tis praise to do not what we can but should' alludes to Seneca's advice at *Octavia* 454: 'it is praiseworthy to do what is fitting, not just what you can' (*id facere laus est quod decet, not quod licet*). Marston further emphasizes his combination of these two Roman texts by situating Piero and Pandulpho's debate in Act 2, the position occupied by the equivalent debates in *Thyestes* and *Octavia*.

This brief review of Marston shows, once again, how *Octavia*'s reception is intertwined with that of Seneca, and how the play's own reception *of* Seneca proves particularly influential with Renaissance dramatists. Alongside the interrelated genres of tragedy and historical drama, however, is the parallel tradition of 'Roman plays', where *Octavia*'s legacy tends to be more diffuse, employing but also reaching beyond the *praetexta*'s Senecan material to incorporate its female figures, its emphasis on the supernatural and its interest in commemoration. This fashion for Roman plays gained momentum across Europe in the late sixteenth and early seventeenth centuries, due in large part to the Flemish scholar Justus Lipsius publishing an edition of Tacitus' works in 1574 followed by a commentary on the *Annals* in 1581. Lipsius' full edition of Seneca's philosophical prose emerged in 1605, and these publications, alongside his advocacy of Neo-Stoicism,[25] created fertile intellectual ground for exploration of the pseudo-Senecan *Octavia*. The *praetexta*'s influence in the English tradition of Roman plays is most strongly apparent in Matthew Gwinne's sprawling *Nero: A New Tragedy* (1603), which the author dedicated to Lipsius; Ben Jonson's *Sejanus* (1603); Thomas May's *The Tragedy of Julia Agrippina* (1628); and Nathaniel Richards' *The Tragedy of Messalina* (1639). In the French tradition, which I will consider for the remainder of this section, fascination for dramatizing Julio-Claudian history took root a little earlier, with Marc Antoine Muret, whose neo-Latin *Julius Caesar* (1544) was the product of its author's enduring scholarly interest in Seneca (his edition of Seneca's philosophy was published posthumously, in 1587) and Roman history (his commentary on Tacitus' *Annals* also received posthumous publication, in 1604).[26] Although dramatically weak, his *Julius Caesar* is significant both as an early example of French Renaissance Senecanism and for its distinctive treatment of *Octavia*.

Given its author's credentials, Muret's play is remarkable in deviating from the mainstream Renaissance pairing of *Octavia* and Senecan tragedy. This happens chiefly because Muret's Caesar is an ambivalent tyrant, his characterization deriving from Seneca's *Hercules Furens* and the spurious *Hercules Oetaeus* rather than Atreus in *Thyestes*.[27] He is ambitious and self-absorbed but does not engage in amoral violence and is even celebrated in apotheosis at the play's end. This (mildly) more positive portrayal of autocracy renders the *Octavia–Thyestes* intertext unnecessary. Instead, Muret focuses on Poppaea's dream scene (*Oct.* 690–761), which he transforms into a dialogue between Calpurnia and her nurse.

Muret's exchange begins with Calpurnia shaking in fright. She has witnessed a nightmare on the previous evening while embracing Caesar in sleep. Her somnolent pose, 'having clasped my dear Caesar's neck' (*amplexa blandum Caesaris collum mei*, *Caes.* 259), is an obvious allusion to Poppaea's at *Octavia* 716, 'in my Nero's embrace' (*inter Neronis ... complexus mei*), the possessive pronoun in both cases conveying the woman's affection for her spouse. From this peaceful state there ensues a hellish vision: Calpurnia dreams of Caesar prostrate and bleeding profusely from multiple stab wounds (*Caes.* 267–9). Gone are the symbolism and ambiguities of Poppaea's dream, but Muret retains the precise detail of death by stabbing, which, besides its historical accuracy, evokes Nero's culminating appearance in both Poppaea's dream (*Oct.* 732–3) and Octavia's (*Oct.* 121–2). The link to both dreams is further confirmed in line 270 of Muret's scene, where Calpurnia's waking, 'then sudden terror expelled sleep' (*tum mihi quietem subitus excussit timor*), echoes Octavia's at 123 and Poppaea's at 734. One effect of these allusions is to juxtapose Octavia and Calpurnia: the former fears a Caesar while the latter fears *for* Caesar. Another effect is to highlight Poppaea's affection for Nero, which her dream's prophetic violence and her links to Octavia tend to overshadow. Love is a prominent albeit auxiliary theme in Muret's exchange just as in *Octavia*'s.[28] And Calpurnia's concomitant distress at Caesar's fate invites us to interpret Poppaea's less as *fear of* than *concern for* her husband.

This recognition of love's thematic importance in *Octavia*, coupled with appreciation of its focus on female characters, culminates after a lengthy and halting evolution in the elegant power of Jean Racine's *Britannicus* (1669). Though separated from Muret's work by more than a century, Racine's play is very much a part of the French Senecan tradition, which undergoes a resurgence in the 1630s and maintains momentum late into the seventeenth century.[29] Less focused on blood and vengeance than English Senecanism, the French tradition dwells on Senecan introspection and self-formation, and on the 'clash of passion and politics', as well as imitating Senecan style in its long monologues, *sententiae* and ghostly prologues.[30] French tragedy also devotes more attention to love plots,[31] which may be part of the reason for its sustained engagement with *Octavia*.[32] The *praetexta* is certainly one of Racine's sources for *Britannicus*. Although the playwright himself acknowledges only his debt to Tacitus (in his 1670 and 1676 preface), his tragedy is the product of broader contemporary fascination for Julio-Claudian Rome, which included vernacular editions of Tacitus and Suetonius, widespread imitation of Seneca and – most significantly – Pierre Corneill's Roman plays, *Cinna* (1641) and *Othon* (1664), the former of which draws on *Octavia*.[33] Another major cultural influence for Racine was Claudio Monteverdi's 1643 opera, *L'incoronazione di Poppea* ('Poppaea's coronation'), which not only adapts the pseudo-Senecan *Octavia* (see the next section, 'Opera') but also brings its love plot to the fore. *L'incoronazione*'s focus on the marital intrigues of Nero's court provides impetus for Racine portraying Britannicus and Nero as love rivals and framing his contemplation of autocracy in amatory terms.

Britannicus begins with Agrippina complaining of Nero's increasing tyranny and disregard for her, and of her own diminishing power. We learn that Britannicus is in love with a young noblewoman, Junia, whom Nero has abducted on a vague charge of insubordination. Burrhus cautions Agrippina not to intercede, while Britannicus enlists Narcissus to help with Junia's release. The request is futile: Narcissus, two-faced, actually serves Nero, and Nero confesses he has fallen in love with Junia, a sentiment she does not return but with which she is forced to comply. Attempts to dissuade Nero from his plans to divorce Octavia and marry Junia fail. Britannicus, Burrhus and Agrippina all try to temper the tyrant's desires until eventually, on the pretext of reconciliation, Nero poisons Britannicus, leaving Agrippina and Burrhus to lament the future of his rule.

Octavia's influence is present throughout, emerging from plot details and patterns of interaction as well as direct verbal borrowing. Curiously, Octavia herself is absent, but Racine disperses her role across several other characters. Junia, for instance, resembles Claudius' daughter in her tearful fear of Nero and in blaming the emperor for her brother's death (*Brit.* 420). She also, ironically, occupies Poppaea's role in being Nero's latest object of affection. Like Poppaea's, Junia's beauty seems incomparable, and Nero's devotion to her, his willingness even to throw himself at her feet (*Brit.* 606), highlights *Octavia*'s crucial yet overlooked use of love elegy.[34] Further, Junia's subtle combination of Octavia and Poppaea suggests Racine recognized the effect of *Octavia*'s symmetrical dramaturgy. At the very least, he may have been inspired by the doubling and parallel plots of Monteverdi's opera,[35] which owe as much to *Octavia* as they do to Roman comedy.

Besides Junia, Britannicus, too, resembles Octavia in his status as Nero's young, innocent sibling victim, and in the play's insistence on his legitimate claim to imperial power (*Brit.* 856–9). His role finds stronger parallels, however, in the minister/Seneca character from the customary counsellor–tyrant scene, and in the figure of Seneca's Thyestes, whom he resembles in being deceived and ultimately undone by a vindictive, powerful brother. In the first regard, Britannicus echoes *Octavia*'s Seneca, when he confronts Nero and advises mild rulership instead of autocracy (*Brit.* 1041–100). In a dispute that imitates *Octavia* 456–8, Britannicus admonishes Nero that, 'everyone should be glad of a happy reign' (1071) and in response, Nero channels Accius' Atreus: 'Never mind happiness, as long as they fear me' (cf. *Atr.* 203–4 *TRF*²).[36] The scene follows *Octavia*'s model in using the Thyestes myth to interpret this imagined historical encounter. In summoning Accius, Racine also, inevitably, summons Seneca's *Thyestes*, representing Nero as a palimpsest of roles from *Octavia*'s Nero, via Seneca's Atreus, all the way back to Accius; the tyrant's typology has a long dramatic pedigree. It follows that Britannicus plays Thyestes to Nero's Atreus, a connection Racine signals in this same scene by having Junia exclaim at Nero's aggression, 'What are you doing? / It is your brother' (1085–6).

Strong debts to *Octavia* also feature in Act 4 Scene 3, where Burrhus urges Nero to refrain from spilling sibling blood and instead preserve his virtuous reputation. Like Seneca in *Octavia*, Burrhus weaves into his argument passages from Seneca's *On Clemency*: he ventriloquizes Nero reflecting with pleasure on the extent and decency of his power (*Brit.* 1375–80; cf. *Clemency* 1.1.2–4); reminds the *princeps* that he used to spare 'even the meanest blood' (*Brit.* 1382; cf. *Clemency* 1.1.3); and recalls how Nero once wished he could not write to avoid signing a death warrant (*Brit.* 1383–8; cf. *Clemency* 2.1.2, where it is actually Burrhus who brings the warrant to Nero). When Racine's Nero protests this advice – 'Am I to submit to everyone's wishes / Except my own?' (1351–2) – he, too, conflates *Octavia* (esp. 574) with *On Clemency* (1.8.1). The scene's overall effect is like *Octavia*'s: it imbues Seneca's philosophical advice with tragic futility. But in replacing Seneca with Burrhus, Racine aims at a more clear-cut division between vice and virtue, avoiding Seneca's ambivalent reputation in favour of Burrhus's simpler one that allowed more room for invention.

Accompanying these prototypical allusions to *Octavia* is the towering figure of Agrippina, whose inclusion acknowledges the *praetexta*'s remarkable interest in female perspectives. Like her ancient dramatic counterpart, Racine's Agrippina is simultaneously dislikeable and pitiable. Her first appearance is notable for recalling Octavia's in *Octavia* Scene 1: Racine's Agrippina bemoans her present circumstances in the company of a confidante, and remarks of her dwindling influence, 'only the shadow remains' (*Brit.* 117). As an allusion to *Octavia* 71, the line not only invites pity for Agrippina as one of Nero's prospective victims, crushed and sidelined by his tyranny, but also accentuates her moral ambiguity in contrast to Octavia's, because she facilitated the oppression she now suffers. This conflicting portrayal of Agrippina as a cause and casualty of Nero's reign is something Racine inherits from his Roman model: Racine's Agrippina regrets yet remains proud of her manoeuvres to install Nero as emperor (*Brit.* 47–50; 162–3; 850–1; 1135–212; cf. *Oct.* 331–44; 600–13); worries that the *princeps* will 'erase [her] from his memory' (*Brit.* 153; cf. *Oct.* 610–12); and curses him, prophetically, with suicide and posthumous disgrace (*Brit.* 1705–11; cf. *Oct.* 619–31). She is both a mechanism of his power and an illustration of its enduring villainy.

In anticipating Nero's future ruin, moreover, Racine's Agrippina revisits *Octavia*'s emphasis on commemoration and giving Nero's victims a voice. Her hope for Nero's posthumous infamy is, from the audience's perspective, the foregone judgement of history: 'your name will be such that, to posterity / The cruellest tyrants will think it an insult' (*Brit.* 1709–10). Her words cement the play's – and by implication, our – view of Nero, but their real power derives from their being Agrippina's: they show that history will side not with Nero but with those who suffered under his reign. Racine's preservation of this effect is testament to *Octavia*'s dramatic power. It likewise signals the success of *Octavia*'s ideological stance, for it is the *praetexta*'s opinion of Nero that prevails over any popular attempt to rehabilitate his reputation. Agrippina's prophecy is self-fulfilling; Racine understands this and reiterates its impact.

5.2 Opera

Increased interest in *Octavia*'s romantic themes – which we see developing in mid-seventeenth-century French tragedy – finds a parallel in early opera, beginning with Claudio Monteverdi and Giovanni Busenello's *L'incoronazione di Poppea* in 1643. This opera marks the start of a long tradition of operas about Nero, many using the pseudo-Senecan *Octavia* as source material and dramatic inspiration.[37] *Octavia* claims a prominent place in this tradition not just because of its historical content but because its tale of love, betrayal and remarriage fits opera's preoccupation with romance,[38] while its 'Senecan' provenance adheres with the fundamentally Roman qualities of early operatic plots.[39] Further, *Octavia*'s pitting of personal choice against public obligation speaks to the political context of early Italian opera, and more broadly, of late-seventeenth-/early-eighteenth-century Europe.[40] It is only in the later eighteenth century that *Octavia*'s influence on opera begins to recede, perhaps in correlation with Seneca's diminishing popularity as a playwright.[41] Most 'Nero' operas from this period well into the twentieth century focus not on Nero's divorce but on his accession, treatment of Christians and suicide.[42] *Octavia*'s neglect has, however, recently ended, with Michael Hersch and Stephanie Fleischmann's stunning *Poppaea* (2019), a spare, grim modern opera that reworks *Octavia*'s plot to suit a foreboding Senecan aesthetic.[43] Since many of these operas – with the exception of Hersch and Fleischmann's – have received comprehensive treatment in Gesine

Manuwald's 2013 monograph, *Nero in Opera*, I limit the following discussion to the most notable examples.

Any account of *Octavia*'s cultural afterlife must acknowledge Monteverdi and Busenello's *L'incoronazione di Poppea*. This opera tells a tale far more complex than *Octavia*'s, one that features Ottone (Otho) as Poppea's jilted lover; a young noblewoman, Drusilla, who loves Ottone; and a whole cast of subsidiary characters including personifications of Fortune, Virtue and Love. The main plot pivots around Nerone and Poppea's desire to be married: Nerone removes Ottavia as the chief impediment to his happiness, and Poppea removes Seneca as the chief impediment to hers. Divorced and bereft, Ottavia leaves for exile in Act 3 Scene 6, while Seneca, having received the order for suicide, dies in the middle of Act 2. Accompanying these central events is a semi-comic subplot in which Ottavia, having spurned her nurse's advice to avenge herself on Nerone by committing adultery in turn, instead prevails upon Ottone to murder Poppea. Ottone acquiesces despite his love for Poppea and proceeds to attempt the assassination disguised in a dress he has borrowed from Drusilla. When the attempt fails, Drusilla is accused of trying to murder her rival for Ottone's love; rather than implicate Ottone, she claims responsibility, but Ottone appears and admits his guilt. Nerone sends the pair into exile. Upon Ottavia's subsequent departure, Nerone marries Poppea and she is crowned empress.

In both structure and content, Busenello's libretto betrays the influence of the pseudo-Senecan *Octavia*. Like the play, the opera divides neatly into two halves with a central scene focusing on death: Seneca's suicide in *L'incoronazione* and Agrippina's ghost predicting Nero's ruin in *Octavia*.[44] *L'incoronazione* also resembles the *praetexta* in having Ottavia and Poppea occupy parallel scenes, each accompanied by a nurse and each, in this case, discussing the problem of Nero's love affair.[45] Act 1 Scene 4 presents Poppea rejoicing in Nero's love and anticipating imperial power while her nurse, Arnalta, warns her against trusting in the *princeps*' beneficence and constancy. The scene immediately following presents Ottavia, likewise in dialogue with *her* nurse, but this time with the moral perspectives inverted: Ottavia laments her abandonment yet remains steadfastly virtuous in response to her nurse's suggestion of an affair. As in *Octavia*, such dramaturgical symmetry highlights one woman's role as a replacement of the other. But Busenello also develops the idea differently, using parallel scenes to indicate Ottavia and Poppea's dissimilarity rather than, in *Octavia*, their essential sameness.

In terms of content, *L'incoronazione* imitates *Octavia*'s portrait of Nero: a self-centred tyrant who brooks no obstacles to his desires and whose obsessive love for Poppaea induces him to disregard the political and moral perils of his divorce. Both the play and the opera draw attention to love's overwhelming, potentially destructive power, and the clash it provokes between the emperor's private wishes and duties to the state.[46] Yet the opera's portrayal is more one-sided than *Octavia*'s because it removes the backdrop of civil unrest and downplays Nero's need for an heir,[47] which in the Latin drama gives Nero's affair a political slant.

Direct allusions to *Octavia* include Ottavia's farewell to Rome in Act 3 Scene 6,[48] and Seneca's monologue in Act 2 Scene 1, where the philosopher's praise of solitude and joy in studying the heavens echoes his entrance monologue at *Octavia* 381–90. Similarly recognizable citations occur in Act 1 Scene 9, which is yet another reprise of the counsellor–tyrant scene between Seneca and Nero. The exchange's content and stichomythic form echo *Octavia* 455–60 and 581–9 despite only minimal verbal correspondences:

Nerone: La ragione è misura rigorosa
per chi ubbidisce e non per chi comanda.

Seneca: Anzi l'irragionevole comando
distrugge l'ubbidienza.

Nerone: Lascia i discorsi, io voglio a modo mio.

. . .

Seneca: Cura almeno te stesso, e la tua fama.

Nerone: Trarrò la lingua a chi vorrà biasmarmi.

Seneca: Più muti che farai, più parleranno.

. . .

Seneca: Chi ragione non ha, cerca pretesti.

Nerone: A chi può ciò che vuol, ragion non manca.

Nero: Reason is a strict measure
For those who obey not those who command.

Seneca: Rather, unreasonable rule
Destroys obedience.

Nero: Enough of speeches! I want to do it my way.

. . .

Seneca: At least think of yourself and your reputation.

Nero: If anyone blames me, I'll take out his tongue.

Seneca: The more people you silence, the more they'll talk.

. . .

Seneca: He who has no reason must find excuses.

Nero: He who can do what he wants never lacks reasons.

L'incoronazione 1: 9

Octavia's presence in the scene is unmistakeable: Nero equates might with right and threatens violence against potential popular dissent, while Seneca appears as an ineffectual voice of reason, advising cautious, just, rational rule. Like his counterpart in *Octavia*, Busenello's Nero finds Seneca's counsel exasperating. And Busenello's Seneca, for his part, utters sharp, sententious paradoxes worthy of the philosopher-dramatist himself. The libretto clearly makes use of the ancient *praetexta*, though Busenello himself acknowledges only his debt to Tacitus.[49]

This *Octavia* intertext is largely responsible for *L'incoronazione*'s ambiguous tone, its alternation between light-hearted romance and moral seriousness. *Octavia* supplies many of *L'incoronazione*'s darker elements, while conversely, the opera recasts *Octavia* in carnivalesque terms, as a celebration of personal desire and erotic fulfilment against the demands of public responsibility. Above all, Busenello sanitizes *Octavia*'s representation of female victimhood: he omits Agrippina's ghost – despite her monologue's obvious operatic qualities – and avoids acknowledging Octavia's execution in her famous final aria, 'Addio Roma' (3: 6). In fact, *L'incoronazione* tends to avoid purely tragic modes in favour of elegiac ones that focus on love and separation, so that even Octavia's exilic departure is expressed in terms of her affection for Rome. Busenello's libretto amplifies the *praetexta*'s romantic, elegiac potential: the story no longer concentrates on Octavia's divorce but on Nero and Poppea's love affair and the losses it must inflict. This opera celebrates love's triumph over all obstacles. Its concluding optimism is, however, tempered by hindsight in a manner reminiscent of *Octavia*'s extra-dramatic historical perspective, for just as knowledge of Nero's downfall brightens *Octavia*'s darkness so, conversely, knowledge of Nero and Poppea's marriage casts a shadow over *L'incoronazione*'s jubilant final scenes.[50]

Following closely in the Baroque, carnivalesque, semi-comic tradition of *L'incoronazione di Poppea* is Carlo Pollarolo and Matteo Noris' *Il ripudio d'Ottavia* ('Octavia's Divorce'), which premiered in Venice in 1699. In keeping with popular taste of the period, Pollarolo and Noris' opera, like *L'incoronazione*, features a subplot and multiple pairs of lovers. Nerone falls for Popea and orders Ottavia's divorce. Popea, in turn, abandons her spouse, Ottone, to be with the emperor. In the background to this main plot, Volusio, the secretary of state, conspires against Nerone while Tiridate, the Armenian king, and Muziano, Ottavia's fictitious brother, support Ottavia and Popea respectively. When Volusio's conspiracy is discovered, Volusio and Ottone are sentenced to death (the latter wrongly accused). They escape prison, however, and join Ottavia in a new plot to kill Nerone.

Apprehended, Ottavia is now sentenced to death as the rioting Roman populace tears down Popea's statues. The action reaches its climax while the riots threaten the palace: Ottavia is about to die, but Muziano facilitates reconciliation between Ottavia and Nerone, while Popea reunites with Ottone. Volusio, too, is forgiven and marries Aurelia. Everyone is happy, including the Roman people.

Despite its elaborate and improbable sequences of action, Noris' libretto engages with *Octavia* at multiple levels. First, it follows the *praetexta* in situating Nerone and Popea's love affair against a backdrop of civic rebellion: the people obliterate Popea's statues (*Rip.* 3: 1; cf. *Oct.* 682–6 and 794–9) and Nerone condemns Ottavia for causing public unrest (*Rip.* 3: 5; cf. *Oct.* 865–8). This latter detail, in particular, belongs to *Octavia*'s version of events, for in Tacitus it is Poppaea, not Nero, who accuses Octavia of fomenting civil revolt (*Ann.* 14.61). Noris' other debts to *Octavia* include his sympathetic portrayal of Popea as a more timid, gentle figure than her domineering counterpart in Tacitus. Likewise, Popea's elision with the goddess Venus (*Rip.* 1: 2; cf. *Oct.* 695–7) and comparison of Nerone and Ottavia's marriage to Jupiter and Juno's (*Rip.* 1: 2; cf. *Oct.* 46–7; 219–20; 535) evokes *Octavia*'s mythic framework, especially its open acknowledgement of the imperial couple's brother–sister relationship.

Other echoes are less distinct, having been reworked by Noris to fit his fanciful plot: Octavia maintains a close relationship with her brother, but that brother is the live and fabricated Muziano, not the deceased Britannicus.[51] The *praetexta*'s use of dream visions and prophecy also finds faint reflection in Aurelia, Ottavia's confidante, witnessing and reporting a prodigy of the empress's downfall (1: 6), while Volusio's failed assassination achieves an effect similar to Agrippina's predictions about Nero in *Octavia*: it subverts Nero's present success by alluding to his eventual overthrow. Noris, like Busenello, appears to have understood *Octavia*'s layered temporality, in which historical hindsight alters the play's emotional tenor.

As much as Pollarolo and Noris' *Ripudio* epitomizes baroque aesthetics, it also signals the end of an operatic era, as the eighteenth century witnessed the establishment of *opera seria* ('serious opera'), which eschewed the carnivalesque in favour of character development and interrogation of moral choices.[52] Reinhard Keiser and Barthold Feind's *Die Roemische Unruhe. Oder: Die Edelmuehtige Octavia* ('The Roman Unrest, or: The Magnanimous Octavia'), which premiered just six years after *Ripudio* in 1705, falls into this latter category, depiction of Nero's ethical progress being the chief aim of its intricate, historically compressed plot.[53] Feind's libretto features no Poppaea, but Ormoena, the fictitious wife of King Tiridates, takes her place. Nero falls in love with Ormoena and abandons Octavia, ordering her death. In the background, Piso plots an uprising while also declaring his love for Octavia. Octavia attempts suicide, but Piso prevents her; Nero, having witnessed some of this in secret, feels sorry for his wife's plight. Seneca critiques Nero's rulership in Act 3, before rebellion erupts, forcing Nero to flee Rome. While Nero sleeps in the fields, Octavia, on Seneca's advice, appears to him disguised as her own ghost, reproaching him with her murder. Piso's rebellion is suppressed, and Nero returns to Rome desirous of reuniting with Octavia. This is duly achieved, and Tiridates reconciles with Ormoena. Seneca intervenes to save Piso, and the opera ends with a song in praise of love.

Similarities to Pollarolo and Noris' *Ripudio* are readily apparent, notwithstanding Keiser and Feind's 'serious' aims. Once again, the libretto follows the Latin *Octavia* in juxtaposing Nero's private desires with a dissatisfied Roman populace, and in staging a philosophically inflected encounter between Nero and Seneca. It also depicts Ormoena, Poppaea's substitute, as hesitant and fearful, characteristics displayed by *Octavia*'s (and Noris') Poppaea in direct contrast to Tacitus'. But Feind's most striking engagement with the Latin *Octavia* is his recasting of Agrippina's spectral appearance as Octavia's own ghostly impersonation (*Edel. Oct.* 3: 7 and 9). Consciously or not, this move emphasizes

Octavia's semi-spectral role in the Latin drama, her status as a shadow of herself. It also confirms Agrippina's alignment with Nero's other female victims in *Octavia* if, despite her savage ambition, she can be interchanged with her hapless daughter-in-law. The swap allows Octavia to voice her grievance as vengefulness, while implicitly associating Agrippina with the casualties of Neronian oppression. Finally, Feind's transposition evokes stories of Nero imagining himself haunted by his mother's ghost, on the model of Orestes (Suetonius *Nero* 34.4), which the Latin *Octavia* likewise employs as a mythological touchstone.

The three centuries proceeding from Keiser and Feind's *Edelmuehtige Octavia* chart a decline in the Latin *Octavia*'s popularity as operatic source material. While 'Nero' operas continue to be produced, their librettos rely more exclusively on historiographic sources and largely avoid treating Nero's love affairs. This all changes, however, with the 2019 premiere of Michael Hersch and Stephanie Fleischmann's *Poppaea*, a twelve-scene opera depicting the story of Nero's divorce through its three main participants – Nero, Octavia and Poppaea – in addition to some handmaidens and a female chorus. Action is simple, sparse and bleak: after a 'dumb show' representing Poppaea's death, time is rewound three years, and the opera begins with Poppaea lamenting her mother's death. Nero arrives and Poppaea tells him she is pregnant; he proceeds to divorce Octavia but the Roman people rebel. In response, Nero and Poppaea accuse Octavia of adultery. Convicted, Octavia is executed while Poppaea looks on. With Octavia dead, Poppaea tries to purify herself. Time speeds forward and she gives birth, but the child dies at just four months old. Poppaea and Nero's world begins to crumble: Rome burns and the Pisonian conspiracy unfolds. Poppaea is pregnant again, but embittered; she reproaches Nero for his recklessness and he responds with violence, beating her brutally. Dying, Poppaea sings a lullaby to her unborn child.

As this summary demonstrates, Fleischmann's libretto adheres closely to the historical record, especially the sequence of events recounted in Tacitus' *Annals* 14.59–64. The character of Poppaea, likewise, appears to have been based on her Tacitean counterpart, though Fleischmann exaggerates the empress' ambition and bloodthirstiness (and adds a measure of Lady Macbeth). But the libretto also betrays *Octavia*'s influence, particularly in the overlap this opera facilitates between its two main female roles. The opening scene of Poppaea recalling and mourning her mother's death (*Popp.* 1) alludes to Octavia doing the same in *her* opening scene (*Oct.* 1–20). Both women emphasize their personal witnessing of the event (*Popp.* 1: 'I watched you', 'I keep watching'; *Oct.* 16–17) and both mothers die on charges of adultery (ironically, Poppaea's mother was the victim of Messalina). This device of having Poppaea replace *and* replicate Octavia's opening lament not only indicates a shift in the story's title role, but also evokes the *praetexta*'s equation of the two women as versions of each other. In succeeding Octavia, Poppaea assumes a similarly dire fate, a correspondence Hersch and Fleischmann's opera underscores just as much as the pseudo-Senecan *Octavia*, albeit through different methods. The two women represent Nero's present and future victims. Octavia herself acknowledges the correspondence in Scene 9, when she appears to Poppaea as a ghost, following the death of Poppaea's daughter: 'your marriage is as barren as mine.' This partial historical symmetry[54] acquires thematic and dramatic weight as a prediction of Poppaea's unhappy future. Whether or not *Poppaea* derives this trick from *Octavia*, the opera uses it to similar effect.

Other correspondences between *Octavia* and Hersch and Fleischmann's opera include the use of two choruses (*Popp.* 2, where the second, rebellious, chorus echoes *Oct.* 682–6 and 794–6); Octavia's obsessive reflection on the past, especially Britannicus' death (*Popp.* 3, 5); the theme of Octavia as a living ghost (*Popp.* 6); and pervasive references to dreams and spectres. Poppaea witnesses her mother's death repeatedly in dreams (*Popp.* 1) and declares herself 'besieged by visions' in the wake of Octavia's murder (*Popp.* 9), both of which events assimilate her to the *praetexta*'s Octavia (whose recurrent nightmare involves Britannicus: *Oct.* 115–22) and to her own counterpart in the Latin play, tormented by a vision of Agrippina (*Oct.* 721–4). Thematically, these apparitions signal the past's incursion into the present, and align with the opera's broader motif of Octavia and Poppaea recollecting their prior misfortunes. They function extra-dramatically as well, to remind audiences of the need to commemorate Poppaea and Octavia's suffering, alongside Nero's tyranny and the unravelling of Poppaea's ambition. Underneath its harsh and dissonant modernism, its ritualistic rawness, Hersch and Fleischmann's opera offers a cautionary tale similar in spirit to *Octavia*'s, namely, that the abuses of Nero's reign must not be forgotten, and that women's domestic experience of his principate deserves a place in collective memory. If anything, *Poppaea* merely accentuates the monstrosity, and ends not with a bang but with a whimper.

Octavia's afterlife is testament to its theatrical and literary worth. Its innovative dramaturgy, alongside its combination of historical and tragic modes, critical handling of Seneca and prominent female voices are all key to its enduring fascination. Equally significant is its position at the dwindling end of various dramatic traditions: *Octavia* is a late, close to final, arrival in the genres of *praetexta* and Roman tragedy, while also recalling major features of classical Athenian tragedy. Perhaps appropriately for a history play, its chief mode of expression is reflective, not only of past events, but of prior theatrical forms, which it resurrects to adapt, interrogate and reimagine. In this respect, it is a perfect source of inspiration for the subsequent reimagining of classical drama in and around the Renaissance period. Its creative, interpretive response to ancient theatrical traditions provided a blueprint for later dramatists and, in following centuries, librettists, who themselves aspired to revisit and revivify Graeco-Roman drama. Though it occupies the margins of Latin literary canons, it is very much at the centre of dramatic and operatic performance across a timespan of more than four centuries – a remarkable and emblematic distinction that is also richly deserved.

Chronology

4 BCE–1 CE	Seneca born in this period
14 CE	Tiberius becomes emperor
31 CE	Seneca enters the Senate
37 CE	Caligula becomes emperor
***c.* 40 CE**	Octavia born to Claudius and Messalina
41 CE	Caligula assassinated
	Claudius becomes emperor
	Seneca exiled to Corsica
	Britannicus born to Claudius and Messalina
48 CE	Messalina executed
49 CE	Agrippina marries Claudius
	Seneca recalled from exile
50 CE	Nero adopted as Claudius' heir
54 CE	Nero becomes emperor
55 CE	Death of Britannicus
April/May 62 CE	Nero divorces Octavia
June 62 CE	Nero marries Poppaea
	Octavia exiled and killed
65 CE	Seneca commits suicide
67/68 CE	Vindex revolts against Nero
68 CE	Galba revolts against Nero
	Nero commits suicide
June 68–Jan 69 CE	Galba emperor
	Octavia composed?
Jan–April 69 CE	Otho emperor
April–Dec 69 CE	Vitellius emperor
Dec 69 CE	Vespasian becomes emperor
70s CE	*Octavia* composed?

79 CE	Titus becomes emperor
81 CE	Domitian becomes emperor
Early 90s CE	*Octavia* composed?
96 CE	Domitian assassinated

Guide to Further Reading

Literary appreciation of *Octavia* has only recently gained momentum, in the first few decades of the twenty-first century. The play's rising stock in Anglophone scholarship is partly due to the publication of two superb high-level commentaries, by Rolando Ferri (2003) and Tony Boyle (2008), which have facilitated more nuanced and widespread study of the text. Credit must also be given to Patrick Kragelund, who has spent a lifetime working on *Octavia* and bringing it to the attention of the wider scholarly community. Kragelund (1982) *Prophecy, Populism, and Propaganda in the 'Octavia'* remains a key study in favour of a Galban dating, while his most recent monograph, Kragelund (2015) *Roman Historical Drama: The 'Octavia' in Antiquity and Beyond*, is a more expansive study that situates the play within broader Roman *praetexta* traditions. The other notable Anglophone monograph on the play is Ginsberg (2017) *Staging Memory, Staging Strife: Empire and Civil War in Octavia*. This fundamentally intertextual study examines how *Octavia* reworks Augustan and Neronian literature and thereby engages in processes of cultural memory. Fruitful treatment of the play can also be found in Wilson (2003) *The Tragedy of Nero's Wife: Studies on the* Octavia Praetexta, which comprises an insightful collection of essays by prominent scholars of Roman drama.

In terms of individual articles / book chapters, Herington (1961) '*Octavia Praetexta*: A Survey' is a trailblazing piece that provides an excellent overview of the play's main scholarly issues; it remains crucial reading. In the case against Senecan authorship, Carbone (1971) 'The *Octavia*: Structure, Date and Authenticity' has been decisive. More recent highlights in *Octavia* scholarship include Smith (2003) 'Looking Back with *Octavia*', a shrewd synoptic analysis that argues strongly in favour of the play's literary and dramatic value; Geue (2019) *Author Unknown*, a large section of which is devoted to exploring the interplay of names, namelessness, and power in *Octavia*, and clearly draws inspiration from Smith; and Bexley (2017) 'Double Act: Reperforming History in the *Octavia*', which maps the play's obsession with historical repetition onto theatrical processes of re-iteration and resurrection. Overall, the last few decades of scholarship on *Octavia* have been characterised by a willingness to treat the play's quirks or previously perceived deficits as significant and richly rewarding interpretive material, regardless of whether the playwright conceived of them as such.

Moving beyond *Octavia* to the contextual realm of Roman historical drama, Manuwald (2001) *Fabulae praetextae. Spuren einer literarischen Gattung* is a useful overview, as is the material collected in Kragelund (2002), a special issue of *Symbolae Osloensis* containing a long essay by Kragelund himself, on the development and distinguishing characteristics of Roman *fabulae praetextae*, followed by brief critical responses from other scholars. Wiseman (1998) *Roman Drama and Roman History* maintains that *preatexta* traditions were more fundamental to early Roman cultural development and more widespread than surviving evidence implies. Though it has not gained wide acceptance, the view has been invaluable in forcing scholars to question their preconceptions of the genre.

For historical context, Barrett (1986) *Agrippina* is a formidably detailed and well-researched biography, an informative source of background information on *Octavia*'s imperial gender politics. For Nero, major works include Griffin (1984) *Nero: The End of a Dynasty*; Champlin (2003) *Nero*, an influential revisionist study that argues for a rationale underpinning Nero's flamboyant activity; and Drinkwater (2019) *Nero: Emperor and Court*, which examines Nero in the context of Roman government: imperial court, Senate, and wider administration.

Octavia's reception in opera is well covered by Manuwald (2013) *Nero in Opera*, a comprehensive study focused chiefly on source criticism. Articles by Rosand (1985) 'Seneca and the Interpretation of *L'incoronazione di Poppea*' and Ketterer (2003) 'Why early opera is Roman and not Greek' are useful interpretive supplements to Manuwald's catalogue-style approach. *Octavia*'s influence on proto-Humanist, Renaissance and Early Modern drama is less well documented. The final chapter of Kragelund (2015) sketches some lines of influence, as does Boyle in the Introduction to his 2008 commentary. Wilson (2003) lists a range of plays that draw on *Octavia*. Useful if scattered observations can also be found in studies about the afterlife of Senecan drama, notably Braden (1985) *Renaissance Tragedy and the Senecan Tradition*, and Perry (2020) *Shakespeare and Seneca Tragedy*, alongside the collation of allusive excerpts in Cunliffe (1965) [1893] *The Influence of Seneca on Elizabethan Tragedy*.

Notes

1 *Octavia* and Roman Historical Drama

1 See Ferri (2003) 75–82 for an account of *Octavia*'s textual transmission.

2 Carbone (1977).

3 The fullest overview of these stylistic differences is Ferri (2003) 31–54. See also Helm (1934); Herington (1961) 26–7; Junge (1999) 221–72; and Boyle (2008) xiv.

4 Sullivan (1985) 72–3.

5 First proposed by Ritter (1843). See also Mattingly (1959) 106–7.

6 Boyle (2008) xvi.

7 Kragelund (1982) 38–52 and (2015) 297–360. See also Barnes (1982) and Wiseman (2004) 264–5.

8 Junge (1999), 199–200; Smith (2003), 426–30; Boyle (2008) xiv–xvi.

9 Proposed chiefly by Ferri (2003) 16–27.

10 On Galba's coinage, see Kragelund (1982) 38–52 and (2015) 314–25. On Nero's *luxuria*, Kragelund (2000).

11 Champlin (2003) 9–12.

12 As summarized by Martial, *On the Spectacles* 2.11–12: 'Rome has been restored to herself and with you in charge, Caesar, the delights that once belonged to a master now belong to the people' (*reddita Roma sibi est et sunt te praeside, Caesar, / deliciae populi, quae fuerant domini*).

13 Suetonius *Life of Vespasian* 18. Tacitus (*Histories* 1.3) admits to having begun his career under Vespasian, presumably benefitting from the emperor's support. Josephus' *Jewish War* was also written under Vespasian's patronage.

14 Helm (1934) 283–347.

15 Ferri (2003) 17–27.

16 Mainly by Junge (1999) 281 n.904 and Kragelund (2015) 299–300.

17 Ferri (2003) 25.

18 Ferri (2003) 9–16; Beck (2007) 15. See also Helm (1934) 326. The approach is disputed by Kragelund (2015) 301–3.

19 Ferri (1998).

20 Goldberg (2003) considers the interpretive problems posed by *Octavia*'s anonymity.

21 Geue (2019) 80–114. Though Geue's own attempt to argue for the play's deliberate anonymity is itself a species of the historicizing interpretation he tends to dismiss.

22 I cite post-structuralism advisedly, despite the reviewer's reservations about its supposed disciplinary obsolescence. Quite the contrary: Geue's radical approach to *Octavia* is post-structuralist in origin, as are most studies of intertextuality and reception that proliferate in the field of Latin literature. Though the movement itself is rarely discussed nowadays, its influence on late twentieth- and early twenty-first-century Classics remains foundational.

23 Barthes (1977) 142–8.

24 For instance, Tarquin's dream in Accius' *Brutus* 17–28 *TRF*^{2} clearly alludes to Atossa's in Aeschylus' *Persians* 176–225. See Boyle (2008) 244 for further discussion.

25 See Rosenbloom (2006) on Aeschylus' *Persians* as both a celebration of Athenian pride and a warning to Greek audiences about the dangers of imperial overreach.

26 An interrelationship that became more intense as the genres developed: see Hattaway (2002) 3–10 on the similarities between Shakespeare's tragedies and historical dramas.

27 See Manuwald (2011) 156–69 for an overview of the *fabula togata*.

28 Manuwald (2011) 142.

29 Noted by Manuwald (2011) 142 and explored more fully by Kragelund (1982) and (2015).

30 See Goldberg (1996); Beacham (1991) 125–53.

31 Lists of possible titles are given by Flower (1995) 189 and Kragelund (2002) 12.

32 The main proponent is Wiseman (1994) 1–22 and (1998). For refutations, see Flower (1995) 173–5 and Manuwald (2001) 91–4.

33 Naevius appears to have introduced new material to Roman tragedy, practiced *contaminatio* prior to Terence, used the 'clever slave' figure

prior to Plautus and cemented Roman drama's political involvement: see Manuwald (2011) 194–204 and Boyle (2006) 36–55.

34 It is generally assumed that *Romulus* and *Lupus* are the same work: see Kragelund (2002) 14; Boyle (2006) 52.

35 Kragelund (2002) 26–7 makes a valiant attempt.

36 This information rests on Varro *On the Latin Language* 6.7 and 7.72, but the passages' validity is disputed.

37 Herington (1961) 24–5.

38 Except for Seneca's *Troades* and incomplete *Phoenissae*, where dramatic action occupies several locales.

39 Ribbeck (1962) attributes the first of these three fragments to Cassius' rather than Accius' *Brutus*, but his construal of Varro *On the Latin Language* 6.7 is incorrect.

40 Boyle (1983); Segal (1986) 115–29.

41 The *Electra* intertext was first noted by Hosius (1922).

42 For example, Beare (1964) 236; Dupont (1985) 227.

43 Marshall (2002) 75.

44 See Ginsberg (2015).

45 A useful summary of this complex debate is Liapis, Panayotakis and Harrison (2013) 29–31.

46 Here I argue against Ferri (2003) 54–69.

47 Dupont (1997) 48; Gurd (2012) 105–26.

48 Flower (1995) and Kragelund (2002). The view that *praetextae* were performed at triumphs and funerals – see e.g. Dupont (1985) 218–24 – has few supporters now.

49 On Paullus' preference for lavish entertainment, see Polybius 30.14 and Livy 45.32. Flower (1995) 183–7 is the main source of these hypotheses about *praetextae*'s performance context.

50 Ovid *Fasti* 4.326 alludes to a performance at the *Megalenses* of Claudia Quinta introducing the Magna Mater's cult to Rome, but it may not be a *praetexta*; see Marshall (2002) 78. The other is a play about the *Nonae Caprotinae*, mentioned by Varro in *On the Latin Language* 6.18.

51 Proposed by Wiseman (2004) 264–5.

52 Bexley (2015) 779–83.

53 Hanses (2021) 63–94 is particularly informative on revival performances of comedy. See also Bexley (2015) 777–8, esp. n.16.
54 Wiles (1991) 132.
55 A prospect dismissed indirectly by Wiles (1991) 130 but entertained by Flower (1996) 114–15 and Slater (1996) 36–9.

2 Historical Background

1 Whitman (1978) 124–5; Ferri (1998); Billot (2003); Taylor (2010).
2 Ferri (1998) 341 and 347–8.
3 Tacitus' Julia Livilla (Agrippina's sister, exiled to Pandateria in 41/2 CE) may also be a misreading of Julia Livia (mother of Rubellius Plautus, executed or committed suicide 43 CE), mentioned at *Octavia* 944–6. The similarity of the women's names and fates, along with the significant location of Julia Livilla's exile, may have prompted Tacitus to exchange one name for the other.
4 Ferri (1998) 348–53.
5 Chronology given by Kragelund (2015) 178–83, esp. n.16.
6 Calculated from Nero's death, which occurred on either 9 or 11 June and was said, by Suetonius *Nero* 57.1, to have happened on the anniversary of Octavia's. On the date of Nero's death, see Champlin (2003) 272 n.9.
7 Bexley (2017) 161–7.
8 Griffin (1976) 93–4 and (1984) 81.
9 Griffin (1984) 80–1.
10 A key feature of Senecan drama, noted by Boyle (1983).
11 Smith (2003) 396 calls the *Octavia* 'an interpretative response to Senecan drama' that 'saw in Seneca's mythological plots a reflection of the socio-political climate of the later Julio-Claudian dynasty'. See also Calder (1983) 195.
12 Such reflexive language of self-possession is characteristic of the *Letters* above all. On the coinciding themes of retirement and autonomy in the *Epistles*, see Wilson (2014) 200–2.
13 Billot (2003) 132–3.

14 Schmidt (1985) 1433–4; Poe (1989) 446–7; Billot (2003) 133–4.

15 Thus, Junge (1999) 201.

16 A phenomenon addressed, superbly, by Bartsch (1994) 1–35.

17 There is also a lacuna in this paragraph of *Annals* 14, which makes the account even less certain.

18 When two of her brothers didn't. See Drinkwater (2019) 32.

19 Thus Drinkwater (2013) 156: 'there can be no doubt that, even allowing for the habitually neglectful parenting of aristocratic societies, Nero experienced an unusually disturbed childhood'.

20 Barrett (1996) 63–70.

21 Barrett (1996) 86–8. Though accounts are doubtless inflated by ancient gender biases, Messalina does appear to have antagonized the senatorial elite and deployed criminal law against them to an unprecedented extent; see Bauman (1992) 167–76 and Barrett (1996) 103–4.

22 See Barrett (1996) 101–2 for discussion of the legislation and sources.

23 See Ginsburg (2006) 107–12 on Agrippina's stereotype as the *saeva noverca*.

24 See Barrett (1996) 111 on Claudius securing his succession through Nero's adoption. Lindsay (2009) 201 attributes Britannicus' poor status to Messalina's downfall, while Drinkwater (2018) 34 more sensibly makes it a result of her antagonism towards the senate.

25 For example, Augustus used them for Gaius and Lucius.

26 As noted by Ferri (2003) 195.

27 This trend of calling Nero 'Ahenobarbus' must also be distinguished from more official forms of ambivalence about his nomenclature. It is true that even after his adoption, inscriptions in Nero's honour tended to stress his Julian descent while minimizing if not omitting his newly acquired adoptive kinship to Claudius. But highlighting one aspect of Nero's lineage is not the same as disputing it; 'Ahenobarbus' implies membership of a different family and is meant as an insult, not a mark of esteem.

28 Boyle (2008) 130.

29 Ginsberg (2011).

30 Other pertinent uses of *ingens* are *Octavia* 147 and 605.

31 *Genetrix* is used four times for Messalina (10; 102; 258; 536), while *mater* is not used at all. Agrippina's treatment is more balanced: *genetrix* four

times (153; 635; 722; 909) and *mater* six (93; 243; 362; 597; 610; 645). Significantly, Octavia likewise uses *genetrix* to refer to Poppaea's pregnancy at 188, thus emphasizing biological relationships over the looser, social role of *mater*.

32 Evidence in Ferri (1998) 349.

33 Parallels noted by Ferri (1998) 349–51.

34 See e.g. Seneca *On Clemency* 1.1.2–3 and 1.8.3–5.

3 Themes

1 Explored most fully by Ladek (1909).

2 Ferri (1998) 943–6. See also Ballaira (1974) 168–9.

3 Ferri (1998) 946.

4 The situation is further complicated by the received text of Euripides' *Iphigenia in Aulis*: the ending in which Diana rescues Iphigenia seems unlikely to have come from Euripides himself. But the motif of her rescue had currency in early imperial Latin literature: see especially Ovid *Tristia* 4.4.61–82 and *Letters from Pontus* 3.2.45–96, which, according to Boyle (2008) 292, have influenced the *Octavia* passage. This currency is enough for the myth to be taken as a broadly tragic motif, especially in the context of *Octavia*'s general saturation with Greek tragic models.

5 Octavia's virginity is emphasized through association with Astrea at 424 and hinted at in Nero's later claim (537) that her heart has never been joined with his.

6 Boyle (2008) 292.

7 Though, according to Harrison (2003) 120, the parallel imagines Octavia as 'the person who would have sacrificed, if possible, her brother Orestes/Nero'.

8 The allusion is discussed by Boyle (2008) 115–16; Buckley (2013) 149–50; and Ginsberg (2017) 26–31. For the *magnus* pun, see Feeney (1986).

9 On Pompey's immobility in Lucan's epic, see Rosner-Siegel (1983).

10 Ginsberg (2013) 642.

11 A key idea in Ginsberg (2013) and (2017).

12 Ginsberg (2013) 656–66.

13 Wiseman (2004) 267.

14 Boyle (2008) 116. Ginsberg (2013) 647 suggests 'Caesar' instead, but this seems less likely given that 'Caesar' was not a part of Octavia's *own* name and would thus invalidate the Lucanian idea of Octavia being simultaneously a shadow of herself and of her family's reputation.

15 Ginsberg (2017) 82.

16 See Ferri (2003) 264, with valid caveats; Boyle (2008) 193; Ginsberg (2017) 68.

17 Buckley (2013) 140–1; Ginsberg (2017) 69–70.

18 Buckley (2013) 141; Ginsberg (2017) 71–2.

19 Despite the remainder of the *Aeneid* repeatedly questioning that optimism.

20 See Ferri (2003) 271–2 for comparanda.

21 The passage's Lucanian qualities are explored most fully by Buckley (2013) 141–3 and Ginsberg (2017) 96–8.

22 A central argument in Buckley (2013) and Ginsberg (2017).

23 Buckley (2013) 138.

24 Editions that employ Lipsius' emendation include Viansino (1965); Zwierlein (1986); Ferri (2003); and Fitch (2004).

25 Boyle (2008) 290.

26 As done by Giardina (1966); Ballaira (1974); Whitman (1978); and Boyle (2008). *Phariae* is also the preferred reading for Smith (2003) 429; Buckley (2013) 151; and Ginsberg (2013) 646–7.

27 Boyle (2008) 290. Ferri (2003) 402 makes an uncharacteristic error in glossing Nero's remark at *Octavia* 875 as 'a remote island' and discounting Egypt as lacking islands. This looks like another case of Tacitus' narrative overshadowing *Octavia*'s content: Nero says *litus,* not *insula*, at 875.

28 Williams (1994) 191.

29 The bulk of *Octavia*'s Senecan intertexts are charted by Bruckner (1976) and Boyle (2008). See also Herington (1961) 28; Calder (1983) 192–5; Poe (1989); Williams (1994); and Star (2017) 120–5.

30 Parallels noted by Calder (1983) 193–5 and Boyle (2008). See also Manuwald (2003).

31 Boyle (2017) 187 is surely right in seeing Accius' *oderint dum metuant* behind Atreus' *quod nolunt velint*.

32 For the political connotations of Roman tragedies about Atreus, see Davis (2015).

33 Calder (1983) 195.

34 Bruckner (1976) 40–127. See also Poe (1989) 450–1 and Cordes (2022) 301–2.

35 Williams (1994) 185.

36 Calder (1983) 194 and Boyle (2008) 262–72 trace these allusions to *Thyestes*.

37 Likewise, Nero's exclamation *et hoc sat est?* at 848.

38 Ferri (2003) 375.

39 Boyle (1983) 200–2 and explored regularly since.

40 Boyle (2008) 107; 126, and Ginsberg (2013) 644.

41 On reciprocity and revenge, see Kerrigan (1996) 6 and Burnett (1998) 3.

42 Boyle (2008) 148. On Julius Vindex's rebellion, see Drinkwater (2019) 389–406.

43 Connections drawn decisively by Carbone (1977) 52–7.

44 The passage's arrangement is disputed: I follow Boyle (2008) 159–60 in keeping the *A* manuscript reading rather than the transposed order adopted by Zwierlein (1986) and Fitch (2004).

45 The full story is in Livy 3.44–58. See also Boyle (2008) 158–9 and Kragelund (2015) 208–9 for the vignette's significance.

46 Kragelund (2015) 209. Geue (2019) 92 notes in addition the thematic importance of father–daughter bonds in Verginia's and Octavia's stories.

47 *Octavia*'s symmetries are explored further by Bexley (2017) 161–7. For *Oct.* 193–200, I join Boyle (2008) 121 and 137, and Fitch (2004) 534 n.13, in interpreting the *famula* as Acte, against Giancotti (1954) 78; Ballaira (1974) 22; and Ginsberg (2019) 227 n.22 who read it as referring to Poppaea.

48 Woods (2009) 79–80.

49 See Charles (2014).

50 Lucas (1921) 22; Herington (1961) 21; Sutton (1983) 9–19; Schmidt (1985) 1448; Wiseman (1998) 53; Smith (2003) 403–5.

51 Especially by Herington (1961) 21.

52 Smith (2003) 404.

53 As observed by Lucas (1921) 92; Kragelund (1982) 26–34; Sutton (1983) 16–17; and Smith (2003) 414. Note, however, the valid caveats of Carbone (1977) 60.

54 See Manuwald (2001) 292–6 and Smith (2003) 419–20 on the choruses' composition and location. Their contrasting positions outside and inside the palace are also key to the drama's representation of interior space, well analysed by Smith (2003) 412–16.

55 Noted by Van Noorden (2014) 276 n.57

56 Carbone (1977) 50–7.

57 See Hallett (1977) on the Renaissance tragic ghost's relationship to justice and vengeance.

58 Braund 2013; Slaney (2015) 32.

59 With the caveat that accidents of survival may skew our view of ghosts' importance in Greek tragedy: see Hilton (2020) 381–2.

60 Boyle (2011) 238 likens Creon's speech at *Oed.* 530–658 to a messenger's report.

61 On myth as a 'habit of mind' in Neronian Rome, see Herington (1961) 19–20 and Harrison (2022) 387–8.

62 There are lexical similarities, too: see Kragelund (1982) 12–13.

63 Carbone (1977) 59–60.

64 An approach pioneered by Carbone (1977) 62–4 and now generally accepted. Further corroborating the prophetic quality of Poppaea's dream is the nurse's subsequent interpretation, which assumes that this night-time vision conveys information about the future.

65 On the combination of wedding and funeral imagery at *Oct.* 718–23, see Kragelund (1982) 9–10 and Boyle (2008) 246.

66 The story's veracity is questionable, given the trope of tyrants kicking wives (e.g. Cambyses in Herodotus 3.32).

67 See Ferri (2003) 331.

68 Kragelund (1982) 11–14 treats the question in depth.

69 Ambiguity between Crispinus and Nero also fits within the play's theme of doubles and substitutes, by allowing overlap between Poppaea's former and current husband: see Bexley (2017) 165–6.

70 The confused temporality of ghosts is analysed neatly by Robson (2019) 54–5.

71 Auden 'Secondary Epic' (1959)

72 An aspect of all theatrical performance – see Carlson (2003) and Rayner (2006) – but more pronounced here given the subject matter.

73 Mazzoli (2000) 211–12.

74 Reading *lux* rather than *nox* at *Oct.* 20: see discussion in Mazzoli (2000) 208–9.

75 Note the temporal marker provided by the chorus at 669–70: *en illuxit . . . / . . . dies.*

76 Further discussion in Sumi (2002).

77 The main study is Flower (1996) 185–222. On the underexplored role of women's *imagines* in the Roman *atrium*, see Webb (2017) 148–65.

78 See Bexley (2017) 175–80 for further discussion of *imagines* and ghosts in *Octavia.*

79 Smith 2003: 400–1.

80 Ballaira (1974) 129 notes the connection to *effigies* at *Oct.* 794 and Tac. *Ann.* 14.61. Ferri (2003) 319 interprets the passage as referring to a Nero–Poppaea statue group.

81 Ginsberg (2017) flags the importance of memory in *Octavia* but approaches the topic differently from me, in textual/intertextual terms.

82 While Ferri (2003) 153 interprets *Oct.* 96 metaphorically, Boyle (2008) 120 is surely right in connecting this to *Octavia*'s broader thematic interest in monuments and inscriptions.

83 I read *memores mei* at *Oct.* 611 with Fitch (2004), against Ferri (2003) and Boyle (2008).

84 The major study is Flower (2006). On the perils of using the term *damnatio memoriae*, see Champlin (2003) 29–30.

85 Flower (2006) 190–4.

86 Boyle (2008) 238.

87 See Varner (2004).

88 A position adopted most strongly by Kragelund (1982) 38–41, but also featuring in more recent works such as Geue (2019) 113.

89 Ladek (1891) 24–6 and Herington (1977) 276 note the possible connection with a shrine to Ceres, erected by an Acte in 65 CE (*CIL* 11.1414), but the hypothesis is weak.

90 Flower (2006) 160–96.
91 Boyle (2008) 283–4.
92 See Boyle (2008) 284–5 for sources and discussion.
93 Boyle (2008) 287 with comparanda. For inscriptions referring to Agrippina, see the helpful list in Barrett (1996) 219–24.
94 Ferri (2002) 64–5 argues that the play's focus on a central female figure aligns it more with the genre of tragedy than with the *fabula praetexta*.
95 Hind (1972) discusses the allusion to Seneca's *Oedipus*. Similar phrases are attributed to Agrippina in Tacitus' *Annals* 14.8 and Dio 61.13.5, though it is unclear whether they derive from *Octavia* or represent broader appropriation of tragic motifs. For the phrase/theme's tragic background, see Baltussen (2002).
96 Boyle (2008) 245, and also Billot (2003) 129–30.
97 At *Oct.* 739, Poppaea seems to worry not just about the dream's *meaning* but for the safety of her *coniunx*, whether Nero or Crispinus.
98 As discussed by Leigh (1997) 179–84.
99 The only other possible male victim accorded a speaking role is the praetorian prefect, who could represent Faenius Rufus, the prefect who succeeded Burrus in 62 CE and held office alongside the notorious Tigellinus. Rufus was removed in 65 CE, a casualty of Nero's response to the Pisonian conspiracy (see Tacitus' *Annals* 14.57). *Octavia*, however, is silent about any contextual details that could help decipher the prefect's identity.
100 For Tacitus' portrait, Dyson (1970) remains a perceptive and authoritative account.

4 Language, Structure and Style

1 Herington (1961) 24–6; Ferri (2003) 35.
2 Richter (1862) cited by Ferri (2003) 31 n.75.
3 Examples come from Herington (1961) 26 and Ferri (2003) 36. Helm (1934) is the foundational study of *Octavia*'s language and the source of many of these lexical statistics.
4 A note of caution sounded by Zwierlein (1992).

5 See e.g. Bexley (2017) 162–4.

6 Tarrant (1985) 46 notes the thematic significance of *sequor* in *Thyestes*. Mastronarde (1970) and Bexley (2016) discuss *dubitus/dubitare* in Seneca's *Oedipus*.

7 Seneca, by contrast, is a remarkably visual writer. Herington (1966) 443 is instructive on the philosopher-tragedian's 'painter's eye'.

8 Parallels in addition to the passages treated here include *Oct.* 557–65 with *Phaed.* 195–207 and *Oct.* 1–8 with *Herc.* 125–51, the latter examined by Ferri (2003) 35.

9 Tempting as it is to take *senescit* as a pun on Seneca's name, and hence evidence of *Octavia*'s verbal ingenuity, caution must be exercised because the text has been emended: see Ferri (2003) 234–5.

10 Recognized by Boyle (2008) 174.

11 Helm (1934) 317–18; Herington (1961) 26–7; Ferri (2003) 48–9; Smith (2003) 399.

12 See Ferri (2003) 48–9 for comparative discussion of the technique in Ovid, Seneca and *Octavia*. Incidence of disyllabic pronoun/possessive line endings in *Octavia* is 22.5 per cent, disproportionately higher than in Seneca's tragedies.

13 See Boyle (2008) lxxxvii–lxxxviii for clear explanation of *Octavia*'s meter.

14 Ferri (2003) 49.

15 See Geue (2019) 83–5 for fuller analysis of naming conventions in *Octavia*'s first scene.

16 The name's power in Senecan tragedy is a well-established scholarly topic. Fitch and McElduff (2002) is foundational. See also Segal (1982) and Braden (1985) 42.

17 Smith (2003) 398. This hypothesis about performance would not, however, resolve the ambiguities of the nurse's opening speech (*Oct.* 34–56).

18 Geue (2019) 94–102.

19 Geue (2019) 83–93.

20 Tarrant (1978) 227–8 notes the Senecan chorus' 'interlude' quality. The outlier is Davis (1993), who regards Senecan choruses as more integral to the plays' action.

21 Zwierlein (1966) 72–87. Davis (1993) 11–38 tries to establish all choral exits and entries in Senecan tragedy, with mixed results.

22 See Tarrant (1978) 221–2. Seneca's incomplete *Phoenissae* has no choruses, which may imply a process of composition and insertion consequent upon the tragedy's main plot. At the very least, it indicates their detachability.

23 Chaumartin (2002) 59.

24 Ferri (2003) 383 and Tarrant (1976) 285.

25 See Tarrant (1978) 218–21.

26 Boyle (2008) divides *Octavia* into six acts. For an equivalent number of acts in Seneca's *Oedipus*, see Boyle (2011) 98–9.

27 Ferri (2003) 67–8.

28 Although Boyle (2008) lxi wants to read the shorter scenes as representing a deliberate increase in the pace of events, this seems unlikely given *Octavia*'s obsession with balance.

29 As noted by Boyle (2008) lx.

30 Ferri (2003) 60.

31 Ferri (2003) 61.

32 Smith (2003) 413.

33 Boyle (2008) 9.

34 See Tarrant (1978) and Marshall (2000).

35 Smith (2003) 414.

5 Reception

1 A difficult proposition to substantiate given the loss of so many texts, coupled with the challenge of disentangling *Octavia*'s from other versions of history. Nonetheless, Tacitus seems the only surviving Roman author to have adapted material from *Octavia*; it otherwise passes unmentioned, and if not for the play's chance survival in the 'A' branch of Seneca's manuscripts later generations would never have known it existed.

2 Manuwald (2013) 16.

3 This structure, along with the title, indicates Mussato's essentially 'epic' conception of tragedy: it is an *Ecerinid*. See Braden (1985) 102–3 and Grund (2011) xxiii.

4 Kragelund (2015) 365 also notes dramaturgical similarities between the two plays' use of the chorus.

5 Grund (2011) xxi.

6 Kragelund (2015) 372–7.

7 As demonstrated by, for example, Stacey (2007).

8 On *Orbecche*'s legacy, see Braden (1985) 116; Tempera (2015); and Savoye (2018) 14–15.

9 Savoye (2018) 12–13; Di Maria (2017) 128.

10 Correspondences are: *Orb.* 3.3.688–92 and *Thy.* 192–3 (committing an unforgettable atrocity); *Orb.* 3.3.719–20 and *Thy.* 246 (death is not punishment but the end of punishment); *Orb.* 3.3.737–8 and *Thy.* 205–7 (subjects must praise their sovereign's wickedness); *Orb.* 3.3.745–8 and *Thy.* 496 (scarcely able to restrain anger). Sulmone also quotes *Thy.* 545 at 3.4.934–6 (pun about sacrificial victims) and other echoes can be found in Act 4. See Davis (2003) 117–18 for discussion.

11 Braden (1985) 118–21.

12 See Di Maria (2017) 132–7 on the significance of women's suffering and female agency in *Orbecche*.

13 On *Octavia*'s clever reinterpretation of the Senecan tyrant, see Perry (2020) 43–5.

14 Kragelund (2015) 407–13 charts *Octavia*'s pan-European influence.

15 Braden (1985) 105.

16 Seneca's authorship was disputed already in fourteenth-century Italy: see Kragelund (2015) 367–8. There was also the adjacent question of authorship for Seneca's genuine tragedies, whom some believed to have been written by a close relative of the philosopher, but not the philosopher himself: see de Caigny (2011) 39–42.

17 Davis (2003) 90–1 examines *Gorboduc*'s use of *Thyestes*.

18 Full lists of the dramas influenced by *Octavia* are given in Wilson (2003) 2 and Boyle (2008) lxxviii–lxxix.

19 Logan (1969) examines Hughes's use of Lucan. Cunliffe (1965) [1893] 130–55 catalogues the play's extensive borrowing from Seneca/*Octavia*.

20 For comparison, I provide a translation of *Octavia* 583–6 by Boyle (2008) 45, which alludes cleverly to Hughes's appropriation of the scene:

Nero Rumour will call it [i.e. yielding to the people's wishes] defeat.
Sen Rumour's weightless, empty.
Nero It brands many.
Sen It fears high rank.
Nero But carps nevertheless.

21 This is especially true of *Gorboduc*, which draws its material from Geoffrey of Monmouth's *History of the Kings of Britain*.

22 Thus Perry (2020) 45: '*Octavia*'s Nero is a Senecan tyrant subjected to a backward-looking structure of revenge that happens also to be coterminous with the prophetic demands of a happy future.'

23 Davis (2003) 69 and 74 rightly emphasizes the problem of Atreus remaining unpunished at *Thyestes*' end.

24 See Davis (2003) for fuller treatment of *Thyestes*' reception in Act 5 of *Antonio's Revenge*.

25 Lipsius also published his own, 'Senecan-style' *On Constancy* in 1584. See Manuwald (2013) 18–19.

26 See de Caigny (2011) 33–46 on Muret's influence and Claire (2022) for his work on Tacitus.

27 Braden (1985) 124–7.

28 A theme Muret also emphasizes through allusion to Catullus 58: *Caesar meus, nutrix mea, heu, Caesar meus, / Meus ille Caesar, quo mea innixa est salus* (*Caes.* 265–6).

29 Tobin (1971) 47–76. On the 1630s French Senecan revival, see de Caigny (2011) 461–578.

30 Tobin (1971) 12 and 47–76 (quotation from p.75).

31 Tobin (1971) 58.

32 This engagement is often more direct and explicit than the English tradition, e.g. Regnault, *La Tragédie d'Octavie* (1599) and Brisset's translation, *L'Octavie* (1589).

33 Reynolds (2022) 313–14.

34 On *Octavia*'s debt to Roman love elegy, see Ginsberg (2019).

35 A synopsis of *L'incoronazione*'s plot is provided by Manuwald (2013) 40–2.

36 Quotations and line numbers for Racine's Britannicus are from the translation by Sisson (1987). Agrippina, too, likens Nero to Accius' Atreus at *Britannicus* 12–13: 'He has had enough of making himself loved; / From now on his desire is to be feared.'

37 Manuwald (2005) and (2013) surveys the play's influence on opera.

38 Manuwald (2005) 161.

39 See Ketterer (2003) on why opera owes a greater – if often unacknowledged – debt to Roman literature than to Greek tragedy.

40 Rosand (1985) 34 and Ketterer (2009) 1–15.

41 Operatic interest in ancient Rome also dwindles during this period, which likewise accounts for *Octavia*'s receding influence. See Ketterer (2009) 1.

42 See Manuwald (2013) 4.

43 For the definition of 'Senecan aesthetic', see Slaney (2015) 16–38.

44 The idea comes from Manuwald (2013) 42, except that she nominates the Seneca–Nero scene as pivotal, whereas I regard Agrippina's appearance as the centre point of *Octavia*'s structure.

45 Rosand (1985) 42 astutely notes that this material is missing from other historical accounts, thus proving Busenello's reliance on *Octavia*.

46 Though less frequent and immediate than in *Octavia*, popular favour and senatorial discontent still play a role in *L'incoronazione*; see Manuwald (2005) 155.

47 An issue discussed at *Octavia* 532–7 and alluded to at 179–80 and 188.

48 Connections between *Octavia*'s final scene and *L'incoronazione*'s 'Addio Roma' are noted by Rosand (1985) 42 and Kragelund (2015) 416.

49 See Manuwald (2013) 37.

50 A fine observation from Rosand (1985) 34.

51 As noted by Manuwald (2013) 132.

52 Ketterer (2009) 8–10; Manuwald (2013) 23.

53 Manuwald (2005) 158, citing Feind's preface to his libretto.

54 Partial since Poppaea, unlike Octavia, was not childless even though her marriage with Nero failed to produce a surviving heir.

Bibliography

Ballaira, G. (1974), *'Seneca' Ottavia*, Turin: Giappichelli.

Baltussen, H. (2002), 'Matricide Revisited: Dramatic and Rhetorical Allusion in Tacitus, Suetonius, and Cassius Dio', *Antichthon*, 36: 30–40.

Barnes, T. D. (1982), 'The Date of the *Octavia*', *Museum Helveticum*, 39: 215–17.

Barrett, A. A. (1996), *Agrippina: Sex, Power, and Politics in the Early Empire*, New Haven: Yale University Press.

Barthes, R. (1977), *Image, Music, Text*, trans. R. Heath, London: Fontana.

Bartsch, S. (1994), *Actors in the Audience: Theatricality and Doublespeak from Nero to Hadrian*, Cambridge, MA: Harvard University Press.

Bauman, R. A. (1992), *Women and Politics in Ancient Rome*, London: Routledge.

Beck, J.-W. (2007), *'Octavia' anonymi: Zeitnahe praetexta oder zeitlose tragoedia?*, Göttingen: Edition Ruprecht.

Bexley, E. M. (2015) 'What is Dramatic Recitation?' *Mnemosyne* 68: 774–93.

Bexley, E. M. (2016), 'Doubtful Certainties: The Politics of Reading in Seneca's *Oedipus*', in P. Mitsis and I. Ziogas (eds), *Wordplay and Powerplay in Latin Poetry*, 355–76, Berlin: De Gruyter.

Bexley, E. M. (2017), 'Double Act: Reperforming History in the *Octavia*', in R. Hunter and A. Uhlig (eds), *Imagining Reperformance in Ancient Culture: Studies in the Traditions of Drama and Lyric*, 160–83, Cambridge: Cambridge University Press.

Billot, F. (2003), 'Tacitus Responds: *Annals* 14 and the *Octavia*', in M. Wilson (ed.), *The Tragedy of Nero's Wife: Studies on the* Octavia Praetexta. *Prudentia*, 35: 126–41, Auckland: Polygraphia.

Braden, G. (1985), *Renaissance Tragedy and the Senecan Tradition: Anger's Privilege*, New Haven: Yale University Press.

Braund, S. (2009), *Seneca, De Clementia*, Oxford: Oxford University Press.

Braund, S. (2013), 'Haunted by Horror: The Ghost of Seneca in Renaissance Drama', in E. Buckley and M. Dinter (eds), *A Companion to the Neronian Age*, 425–43, Chichester: Blackwell Publishing.

Boyle, A. J. (2006), *Roman Tragedy*, London: Routledge.

Boyle, A. J. (2008), *Octavia: Attributed to Seneca*, Oxford: Oxford University Press.

Boyle, A. J. (2011), *Seneca: Oedipus*, Oxford: Oxford University Press.

Bruckner, F. (1976), '*Interpretationen zur Pseudo-Seneca Tragödie OCTAVIA*', PhD diss., Friedrich-Alexander-Universität Erlangen-Nürnberg.

Buckley, E. (2013), '*Nero Insitivus*: Constructing Neronian Identity in the Pseudo-Senecan *Octavia*', in A. G. G. Gibson (ed.), *The Julio-Claudian Succession: Reality and Perception of the 'Augustan Model'*, 133–54, Leiden: Brill.

Calder, W. M. (1983), '*Secreti Loquimur*: An Interpretation of Seneca's *Thyestes*', in A. J Boyle (ed.), *Seneca Tragicus: Ramus Essays in Senecan Drama*, 184–98, Berwick: Aureal Publications.

Carbone, M. E. (1977), 'The *Octavia*: Structure, Date and Authenticity', *Phoenix*, 31: 48–67.

Carlson, M. (2003), *The Haunted Stage: The Theatre as Memory Machine*, Ann Arbor: The University of Michigan Press.

Champlin, E. (2003), *Nero*, Cambridge, MA: Harvard University Press.

Charles, M. B. (2014), 'Nero and Sporus Again', *Latomus*, 73: 667–85.

Chaumartin, F.-R. (2002), 'Comments', *SO* 77: 57–60.

Claire, L. (2022), *Marc-Antoine Muret, lecteur de Tacite: éditer et commenter Les Annales à la Renaissance*, Geneva: Droz.

Cordes, L. (2022), '*Iuvenis infandi ingeni scelerum capax*: Flavian Responses to Nero's Youth', in M. Heerink and E. Meijer (eds), *Flavian Responses to Nero's Rome*, 287–321, Amsterdam: Amsterdam University Press.

Cunliffe, J. W. (1965) [1893], *The Influence of Seneca on Elizabethan Tragedy*, Hamden: Archon Press.

Davis, P. (1993), *Shifting Song: The Chorus in Seneca's Tragedies*, Hildesheim: Olms-Weidmann.

Davis, P. (2003), *Seneca: Thyestes*, London: Duckworth.

Davis, P. (2015), 'Seneca's *Thyestes* and the Political Tradition in Roman Tragedy', in G. M. W. Harrison (ed.), *Brill's Companion to Roman Tragedy*, 151–70, Leiden: Brill.

de Caigny, F. (2011), *Sénèque le Tragique in France (xvie–xviie siècles): Imitation, Traduction, Adaptation*, Paris: Classiques Garnier.

Di Maria, S. (2017), *The Poetics of Imitation in the Italian Theatre of the Renaissance*, Toronto: University of Toronto Press.

Drinkwater, J. F. (2013), 'Nero and the Half-Baked Principate', in A. G. G. Gibson (ed.), *The Julio-Claudian Succession: Reality and Perception of the 'Augustan Model'*, 155–73, Leiden: Brill.

Drinkwater, J. F. (2019), *Nero: Emperor and Court*, Cambridge: Cambridge University Press.

Dupont, F. (1985), *L'acteur-roi*, Paris: Les Belles Lettres.

Dupont, F. (1997), '*Recitatio* and the Reorganization of the Space of Public Discourse', in T. Habinek and A. Schiesaro (eds.), *The Roman Cultural Revolution*, 44–59, Cambridge: Cambridge University Press.

Dyson, S. L. (1970), 'The Portrait of Seneca in Tacitus', *Arethusa*, 3: 71–83.

Ferri, R. (1998), 'Octavia's Heroines: Tacitus *Annales* 14.63–64 and the *Praetexta Octavia*', *Harvard Studies in Classical Philology*, 98: 339–56.

Ferri, R. (2003), *Octavia: A Play Attributed to Seneca*, Cambridge: Cambridge University Press.

Fitch, J. G. (2004), *Seneca Tragedies II*, Cambridge, MA: Harvard University Press.

Fitch, J. G. and McElduff, S. (2002), 'Construction of the Self in Senecan Drama' *Mnemosyne*, 55: 18–40.

Flower, H. I (1995), 'Fabulae praetextae in context: when were plays on contemporary subjects performed in Republican Rome?' *The Classical Quarterly*, 45: 170–90.

Flower, H. I. (1996), *Ancestor Masks and Aristocratic Power in Roman Culture*, Oxford: Oxford University Press.

Flower, H. I. (2002), 'Roman Historical Drama and Nero on the Stage', *SO* 77: 68–72.

Flower, H. I. (2006), *The Art of Forgetting: Disgrace and Oblivion in Roman Political Culture*, Chapel Hill: University of North Carolina Press.

Geue, T. (2019), *Author Unknown: The Power of Anonymity in Ancient Rome*, Cambridge, MA: Harvard University Press.

Giancotti, E. (1954), *L'Octavia attribuita a Seneca*, Turin: Loescher.

Ginsberg, L. D. (2011), '*Ingens* as an Etymological Pun in the *Octavia*', *Classical Philology*, 106: 357–60.

Ginsberg, L. D. (2013), 'Wars more than Civil: Memories of Pompey and Caesar in the *Octavia*', *The American Journal of Philology*, 134: 637–74.

Ginsberg, L. D. (2015), 'Tragic Rome? Roman Historical Drama and the Genre of Tragedy', in G. M. W. Harrison (ed.), *Brill's Companion to Roman Tragedy*, 216–37, Leiden: Brill.

Ginsberg, L. D. (2017), *Staging Memory, Staging Strife: Empire and Civil War in the* Octavia, Oxford: Oxford University Press.

Ginsberg, L. D. (2019), 'The Failure of Female *Fides* in the Octavia', in A. Augoustakis, E. Buckley and C. Stocks (eds), *Fides in Flavian Literature*, 208–31, Phoenix Suppl. 56. Toronto: University of Toronto Press.

Ginsburg, J. (2006), *Representing Agrippina: Constructions of Female Power in the Early Empire*, Oxford: Oxford University Press.

Griffin, M. T. (1976), *Seneca: A Philosopher in Politics*, Oxford: Oxford University Press.

Griffin, M. T. (1984), *Nero: The End of a Dynasty*, London: Batsford.

Grund, G. R. (2011), *Humanist Tragedies*, Cambridge, MA: Harvard University Press.

Hagmaier, A. (2006), *M. A. Muret, Iulius Caesar, M. Virdung, Brutus*, Munich/Leipzig: K. G. Saur.

Hallett, C. A. (1977), 'Andrea, Andrugio and King Hamlet: The Ghost as Spirit of Revenge', *Philological Quarterly*, 56: 43–64.

Harrison, G. M. W. (2003), 'Forms of Intertextuality in the *Octavia*', in M. Wilson (ed.), *The Tragedy of Nero's Wife: Studies on the* Octavia Praetexta. *Prudentia*, 35: 112–25, Auckland: Polygraphia.

Hattaway, M. (2002), 'The Shakespearean history play', in M. Hattaway (ed.), *The Cambridge Companion to Shakespeare's History Plays*, 3–24, Cambridge: Cambridge University Press.

Helm, R. (1934), 'Die Praetexta "Octavia"', *Sitzungsberichte der Preussischen Akademie der Wissenschaften*: 283–347.

Herington, C. J. (1961), '*Octavia Praetexta*: A Survey', *The Classical Quarterly*, 11: 18–30.

Herington, C. J. (1966), 'Senecan Tragedy', *Arion*, 5: 422–71.

Herington, C. J. (1977), 'Review of Ballaira (1974)', *Gnomon*, 49: 275–9.

Hilton, I. (2020), 'Aeschylean Δίκη and the Undead: Darius as Prophet and Clytemnestra's Revenge', *Classical World*, 113 (4): 381–404.

Hind, J. (1972), 'The Death of Agrippina and the Finale of the *Oedipus* of Seneca', *AUMLA – Journal of the Australasian Universities Language and Literature Association*, 38: 204–11.

Hosius, C. (1922), *Octavia praetexta cum elementis commentarii*, Bonn: A. Marcus und E. Weber's Verlag.

Junge, R. (1999), *Nicholas Trevet und die Octavia Praetexta*, Paderborn: Schöningh.

Ketterer, R. C. (2003), 'Why early opera is Roman and not Greek', *Cambridge Opera Journal*, 15: 1–14.

Ketterer, R. C. (2009), *Ancient Rome in Early Opera*, Urbana, IL: Illinois Press.

Kragelund, P. (1982), *Prophecy, Populism, and Propaganda in the 'Octavia'*, Copenhagen: Museum Tusculanum Press.

Kragelund, P. (2000), 'Nero's *luxuria*, in Tacitus and in the *Octavia*', *The Classical Quarterly*, 50: 494–515.

Kragelund, P. (2002), 'Historical Drama in Ancient Rome: Republican Flourishing and Imperial Decline?', *SO* 77: 5–51.

Kragelund, P. (2015), *Roman Historical Drama: The 'Octavia' in Antiquity and Beyond*, Oxford: Oxford University Press.

Ladek, F. (1891), 'De Octavia Praetexta', *Dissertationes Philologae Vindobodenses*, 3: 3–107.

Ladek, F. (1909), 'Die römische Tragödie *Octavia* und die *Elektra* des Sophokles', *Wiener Eranos*: 189–99.

Leigh, M. (1997), 'Varius Rufus, Thyestes, and the Appetites of Antony', *Proceedings of the Cambridge Philological Society*, 42: 171–97.

Lindsay, H. (2009), *Adoption in the Roman World*, Cambridge: Cambridge University Press.

Logan, G. M. (1969), 'Hughes's Use of Lucan in *The Misfortunes of Arthur*', *The Review of English Studies*, 20: 22–32.

Lucas, F. L. (1921), 'The *Octavia*', *CR* 35: 91–3.

Manuwald, G. (2001), *Fabulae praetextae. Spuren einer literarischen Gattung*, Munich: Beck.

Manuwald, G. (2003), 'The Concepts of Tyranny in Seneca's *Thyestes* and in *Octavia*', in M. Wilson (ed.), *The Tragedy of Nero's Wife: Studies on the* Octavia Praetexta. *Prudentia*, 35: 37–59, Auckland: Polygraphia.

Manuwald, G. (2005), 'Nero and Octavia in Baroque Opera: Their Fate in Monteverdi's *Poppea* and Keiser's *Octavia*', *Ramus*, 34: 152–66.

Manuwald, G. (2013), *Nero in Opera: Librettos as Transformations of Ancient Sources*, Berlin: De Gruyter.

Marshall, C. W. (2000), 'Location! Location! Location!', in G. M. W. Harrison (ed.), *Seneca in Performance*, 27–51, Swansea: Duckworth & Classical Press of Wales.

Marshall, C. W. (2002), 'Comments' *SO* 77: 75–8.

Mastronarde, D. (1970), 'Seneca's *Oedipus*: The Drama in the Word', *Transactions and Proceedings of the American Philological Association*, 101: 291–315.

Mattingly, H. B. (1959), 'The *Domitius* of Curiatus Maternus', *CR* 9: 104–7.

Mazzoli, G. (2000), 'Ombre nell'*Octavia*', in E. Stärk and G. Vogt-Spira (eds), *Dramatische Wäldchen: Festschrift für Eckard Lefèvre zum 65. Geburtstag*, 203–20, Hildesheim: Olms.

Perry, C. (2020), *Shakespeare and Senecan Tragedy*, Cambridge: Cambridge University Press.

Poe, J. P. (1989), '*Octavia Praetexta* and Its Senecan Model', *The American Journal of Philology*, 110: 434–59.

Rayner, A. (2006), *Ghosts: Death's Double and the Phenomena of Theatre*, Minneapolis: University of Minnesota Press.

Reynolds, S. (2022), 'Painting and Silence: Racine and His Classical Sources for *Britannicus* and *Bérénice*', in N. Hammond and P. Hammond (eds), *Racine's Roman Tragedies*, 313–28, Leiden: Brill.

Ritter, G. (1843), *Octavia praetexta*, Bonn: Habicht.

Robson, M. (2019), *Theatre & Death*, London: Bloomsbury.

Rosand, E. (1985), 'Seneca and the Interpretation of *L'incoronazione di Poppea*', *Journal of the American Musicological Society*, 38: 34–71.

Rosner-Siegel, J. A. (1983), 'The Oak and the Lightning: Lucan *Bellum Civile* 1.135–157', *Athenaeum*, 61: 165–77.

Savoye, J.-L. (2018), *Orbecche Tragédie. Édition bilingue italien-français*, Paris: L'Harmattan.

Schmidt, P. L. (1985), 'Die Poetisierung und Mythisierung der Geschichte in der Tragödie Octavia', *Aufstieg und Niedergang der römischen Welt*, 32 (2): 1421–53.

Segal, C. (1982), '*Nomen Sacrum*: Medea and Other Names in Senecan Tragedy', *Maia*, 34: 241–6.

Sisson, C. H. (1987), *Jean Racine: Britannicus, Phaedra, and Athaliah*, Oxford: Oxford University Press.

Slaney, H. (2015), *The Senecan Aesthetic: A Performance History*, Oxford: Oxford University Press.

Smith, J. A. (2003), 'Flavian Drama: Looking Back With Octavia', in A. J. Boyle and W. J. Dominik (eds), *Flavian Rome: Culture, Image, Text*, 391–430, Leiden: Brill.

Stacey, P. (2007), *Roman Monarchy and the Renaissance Prince*, Cambridge: Cambridge University Press.

Star, C. (2017), *Seneca*, London: I. B. Tauris.

Sullivan, J. P. (1985), *Literature and Politics in the Age of Nero*, Ithaca, NY, and London: Cornell University Press.

Sumi, G. S. (2002), 'Impersonating the dead: mimes at Roman funerals', *The American Journal of Philology*, 123: 559–85.

Sutton, D. F. (1983), *The Dramaturgy of* Octavia, Königstein: Anton Hain.

Tarrant, R. J. (1985), *Seneca's Thyestes*, Atlanta: American Philological Association.

Taylor, M. (2010), 'The Figure of Seneca in Tacitus and the *Octavia*', in J. Miller and A. J. Woodman (eds), *Latin Historiography and Poetry in the Early Empire*, 205–22, Leiden: Brill.

Tempera, M. (2005), 'Horror . . . is the sinews of the fable: Giraldi Cinthio's works and Elizabethan tragedy', *Actes des congrès de la Société française Shakespeare*, 22: 235–47.

Tobin, R. W. (1971), *Racine and Seneca*, Chapel Hill: University of North Carolina Press.

Van Noorden, H. (2014), *Playing Hesiod: The 'Myth of the Races' in Classical Antiquity*, Cambridge: Cambridge University Press.

Varner, E. R. (2004), *Mutilation and Transformation*: Damnatio Memoriae *and Roman Imperial Portraiture*, Leiden: Brill.

Webb, L. (2017), 'Gendering the Roman *imago*', *Eugesta – Journal of Gender Studies in Antiquity*, 7: 140–83.

Whitman, L. Y. (1978), *The* Octavia: *Introduction, Text, and Commentary*, Bern and Stuttgart: Haupt.

Williams, G. (1994), 'Nero, Seneca and Stoicism in the *Octavia*', in J. Elsner and J. Masters (eds), *Reflections of Nero: Culture, History & Representation*, 178–95, London: Duckworth.

Wilson, E. R. (2014), *Seneca: A Life*, London: Penguin.

Wiseman, T. P. (1994), *Historiography and Imagination: Eight Essays on Roman Culture*, Exeter: Exeter University Press.

Wiseman, T. P. (1998), *Roman Drama and Roman History*, Exeter: Exeter University Press.

Wiseman, T. P. (2004), *The Myths of Rome*, Exeter: Exeter University Press.

Woods, D. (2009), 'Nero and Sporus', *Latomus*, 69: 73–82.

Zwierlein, O. (1966), *Die Rezitationsdramen Senecas*, Meisenheim am Glan: Anton Hain.

Zwierlein, O. (1986), *L. Annaei Senecae Tragoediae: Incertorum auctorum Hercules [Oetaeus], Octavia*, Oxford: Oxford University Press.

Zwierlein, O. (1992), 'Review of Billerbeck (1988)', *Gnomon*, 64: 502–6.

Index

www.ingramcontent.com/pod-product-compliance
Lightning Source LLC
Chambersburg PA
CBHW070616310726
48982CB00001B/99

9781350121843